CW01668466

' AND DO THE SAME"

STUDIES IN RELATING TO MUSLIMS

by

Colin Chapman

Published jointly by
CHURCH MISSIONARY SOCIETY
and
BMMF INTERNATIONAL
in conjunction with
INTERNATIONAL FELLOWSHIP OF EVANGELICAL STUDENTS

ISBN 0 85273 041 1

*Photoset and printed by Stanley L. Hunt (Printers) Limited,
Rushden, Northamptonshire*

PART I

PART II

RESOURCE BOOKS

INTRODUCTION

The lawyer who asked the simple question "who is my neighbour?" didn't receive a simple answer! He had to work out his own answer from the Parable of the Good Samaritan, and was then told by Jesus "you go and do the same" (Luke 10.25-37).

If the parable taught the Jewish lawyer to see who his neighbour was, and what it meant to love him, it may also teach us as Christians to see Muslims as our neighbours. Whether we are Christians brought up in an Islamic society, expatriates engaged in secular employment or mission work in an Islamic country, or Christians in the west becoming aware of the growing Muslim communities in our midst, the parable should also remind us that loving our neighbour is likely to mean more than simply "sharing the gospel" with him.

It wasn't an accident that Jesus chose as the main characters for the parable people from communities which had strong prejudices against each other. If we as Christians often have the same kind of prejudices towards Muslims as the Jews did towards the Samaritans, we will have to learn that loving our neighbour involves putting aside our prejudices, and doing something very practical to overcome the social, political, cultural and religious barriers which separate us from Muslims.

These studies are no more than an introduction to the subject of Islam and relating to Muslims. They are designed not only to satisfy our curiosity, but also to stir us to action – so that what we learn will lead us to "go and do the same".

SUGGESTIONS ABOUT USING THE STUDIES

1. The studies are designed primarily for *group study.*

2. Part I (1-6) consists of basic studies in Islam, each of which contains material which can probably be discussed in a session of about an hour.

Part II (7-10) deals with more difficult issues, and each study contains more material than can be covered in one session.

3. The section in Studies 1-6 entitled FOR ACTION contains suggestions of practical ways in which members of the group can follow up the study.

The sections entitled FOR FURTHER STUDY can be used at the end of the session if there is sufficient time, or left for each person to study on his own.

4. The leader's task is primarily to select what is most relevant to the group, and guide them through the material and the questions for discussion (Q). For example, he may need to choose some of the Bible and Qur'an passages and omit others; and some of the material which is relevant to Christians living in the Islamic world will mean very little to Christians living in the west, and vice versa.

The leader does not need to be an expert in the subject! It may be helpful for the leader to choose *one book, or two at the most* from each section of the list of Resource Books to help him in his preparation and to pass on to other members of the group.

5. *Each member of the group* should have a copy of the studies, and try to read each study in advance. Each person should also have *a Bible,* and should have access to a *translation of the Qur'an.* (See Resource Books, first section.)

PART 1

1

RELATING TO OUR MUSLIM NEIGHBOURS

We begin at this point because it is essential that we see our study of Islam in the context of our relationships with our Muslim neighbours. Some of us may need to be encouraged to take our first steps in relating to them in a more open and friendly way, while others may need encouragement to go deeper in the relationships we have already established.

1. **Reaching out beyond our own community**

(*Read* Matthew 5.43-48)

Some Pharisees had twisted the OT commandment "love your neighbour" to mean that we should only love people from our own community, and hate our enemies. Jesus teaches here that love is not to be limited in this way.

Q. - If we are really honest with ourselves, what feelings do we have towards our Muslim neighbours? – fear, suspicion? Do we respect them or despise them? Are we friendly, cool or indifferent towards them?

- What are the main reasons why we find it hard to relate to our Muslim neighbours? Is it prejudices in *us* or in *them?*
Is it the political situation in the country?
Is it something in our society?

2. **The Golden Rule** (*Read* Matthew 7.12)

Q. - How would you like your Muslim neighbours to treat you as an individual, and your community?

- How should this affect the way you treat *them?*

- Does it make any difference if the Muslim community is the majority and the Christians are a minority in your country, or the Christians are a majority and the Muslims a minority?

3. **Showing Love in Action** (*Read* Luke 10.25-37)

Jesus answered the question "who is my neighbour?" by telling the parable of the Good Samaritan. He was therefore saying that my neighbour is anyone I meet, anyone I come in contact with – especially if that person is in any kind of need.

Q. – What does this say to me about who are *my* neighbours?

– What does this say about what it means to love my neighbours in practice? Am I prepared to love my neighbours like this?

– What does the parable say about our prejudices? Jesus deliberately chose people from two communities which had strong feelings against each other.

4. **Praying for our Muslim Neighbours** (*Read* 1 Timothy 2.1-6)

Notice the special relevance of this passage to prayer for the Muslim world: the Muslim heartily agrees that "there is one God", but the Gospel goes on to say "there is one mediator between God and men, the man Christ Jesus".

Q. – What is the connection between praying for rulers and for peace (v. 2), and God's desire that everyone should be saved and come to know the truth (v. 4)?

– Why do we believe that we need a mediator between God and men? (*Read* Romans 10.1-2)

Q. – If this is how Paul prayed for his fellow-countrymen, can we pray in the same way for our neighbours – and particularly for our Muslim neighbours?

– How well does Paul's description of the Jews' devotion to God apply to the devotion of Muslims whom we know?

FOR ACTION

1. How can you develop the *natural contacts* you already have with your Muslim neighbours, friends or colleagues at work, etc.? Is there any way in which you can go one stage further in your friendship with them?

Are there any ways in which you can *work* more closely with Muslims – eg, in some form of community service?

2. Is there any other *person or family whom you don't know well* and to whom you could reach out in friendship? (see Matthew 5.46-47).

3. *Greetings* (see Matthew 5.47): What is the commonest form of greeting used by Muslims in your community?

If you are a Christian living in a Muslim community (eg, in the Middle East or Pakistan), is there any reason why you should not use these greetings – at least with Muslims?

If you are a Christian in the West and have contact with Muslims in your community, try to learn and use some of these greetings, eg, the Arabic greeting *issālamu 'alēkum* (peace be upon you) and the reply *wa'alēkum issalām* (and on you be peace).

4. (Particularly for those living in the West.) Find out as much as you can about *the Muslim community in your city and country:*

eg – how many Muslims are there in your city, and in your country?
- what countries do they come from?
- what kind of work do they do?
- where do they live?
- where do they worship and meet?
- if they are a minority, what needs do they feel vis-à-vis the larger, host community?

5. *Visiting:* Find out from a Muslim friend the dates of the major Muslim feasts during the next 12 months (eg, the month of Ramadan, 'Id il Fitr, 'Id il Adha), and the most appropriate time to visit a Muslim family. Note the dates in your diary and make up your mind *now* to visit at least one Muslim family on one of these feast days.

Find out the most appropriate way to visit your Muslim neighbours on important occasions – eg, the birth of a child, a wedding, or a bereavement. Are there any ways in which you can share in these occasions?

6. *Pray* together for the Muslims you know and for the Muslim community in your city and country.

2

UNDERSTANDING OURSELVES AND OUR MUSLIM NEIGHBOURS

Assuming that we are making a real attempt to relate to our Muslim neighbours (Study 1), we now consider some of the questions which are likely to arise as these relationships develop. First, UNDERSTANDING OURSELVES, then UNDERSTANDING OUR MUSLIM NEIGHBOURS.

UNDERSTANDING OURSELVES

1. **Understanding our History and Culture** (*Read* John 4.9)

The Jews disliked the Samaritans –

because of their mixed ancestry
because of their rival temple on Mt Gerizim
because they recognized the OT law but not the Prophets, and
because of the political tension between the two communities over many centuries.

Q. – Is there any parallel between Jewish prejudices towards the Samaritans and Christian prejudices towards Muslims?

– Is it true in our situation to say, "Christians have no dealings with Muslims"? If so, what are the reasons?

2. **Admitting our Suspicious Mentality** (*Read* Acts 9.10-19)

Q. – What were the questions and doubts which must have been raised in Ananias' mind when he heard that Saul had been converted?

– Are they similar to the questions and doubts in *our* minds when we hear of someone from a non-Christian background who is converted?

3. **Admitting our Unbelief** (*Read* Galatians 1.21-24)

Q. – Do we really believe that Muslims can change their minds about Jesus and come to faith in him?

- If someone as prejudiced and hostile as Saul could be converted, is it any harder to believe that a Muslim can be converted?

4. **Admitting our Fear and Praying for Boldness** (*Read* Acts 4.23-31)

Q. - How serious were the threats against the apostles (v. 29)?

- To what extent do we face the same threats today? Is there anything in common between our situation and the situation the apostles were in?
- What did they ask God to do *for them* ? How did God answer their prayer? Are we prepared to ask God for this boldness?
- What did they see as *God's part* in the proclamation of his word?

What part have supernatural evidences (healings, visions, etc.) played in the conversion of any Muslims we know?
Are we prepared to ask God to reveal himself today in miraculous ways?

UNDERSTANDING OUR MUSLIM NEIGHBOURS

1. **The Secret of Genuine Meeting and Dialogue**
(*Read* Luke 2.45-46)

Notice five details in Luke's description of Jesus at the age of 12 in the temple:

he was sitting among the teachers
he was listening to them
he was asking them questions
he had understanding (RSV)
he was giving answers.

Q. - Can this picture help us to see what we must do if we want to have a genuine meeting of minds with Muslims? Our situation may be very different today, since Jesus was relating to his own culture, whereas for many of us Islam represents a religion and a culture which are foreign to us. But are there any principles that we can apply?

a. *SITTING AMONG THEM:*

- How much do we understand about the society to which they belong? about their history and culture?
- Do we know what it feels like to be in their shoes?
- Am I aware of how they react to *me* as a person (because of my colour and nationality; because of the language I speak; because of all the cultural and political factors which affect our relationship)?

b. *LISTENING*

- Am I really willing to listen before I say what I believe?

c. *ASKING QUESTIONS:*

- What kind of questions should we ask to help us to understand?

d. *UNDERSTANDING:*

- What is the difference between knowing about Islam and understanding Islam? between knowing about facts and discernment? between information and insight?
- How do we obtain this kind of insight?

e. *ANSWERS:*

- Are my responses answering the questions in *their* minds or the questions *I* think they ought to be asking?

2. **Knowing 'the Heart of a Stranger'** (*Read* Exodus 22.21, 23.9 and Leviticus 19.33-34)

Q. - Why should the Children of Israel have been in a unique position to understand the feelings of foreigners and immigrants in their community?

- What must it feel like to belong to a Muslim immigrant community in Europe or North America?
- What can Christians in the west learn from these verses about their attitudes and responsibilities towards Muslim communities in their midst?

3. **The Willingness to Identify** (*Read* 1 Corinthians 9.19-23)

Q. - What would it mean to "live like a Muslim"? Is it (a) possible and (b) desirable?

- Does it apply only to the "missionary" living among Muslims? Or could it also be applied to Christians living in the Islamic world?

What would it mean for a foreigner in his relations with Muslims?

What would it mean for a national in his relations with Muslims of his own nationality?

- What is the meaning of verse 23, and how is it related to the question of identification? Is Paul thinking of the blessing he *gives* or the blessing he *receives?*

TEV "All this I do for the gospel's sake, in order to share in its blessings" (cf RSV, NIV).

NEB "All this I do for the sake of the Gospel, to bear my part in proclaiming it."

FOR ACTION

Do something in one or more of the following areas to help you to understand your Muslim neighbours better:

1. Find out some way by which you can *listen* with an open mind to what Muslims in your community are saying today:

eg, by reading magazines, books or tracts (see Resource Books, Books on Islam written by Muslims)

by listening to Muslim radio programmes, or watching TV programmes.

2. Find out all you can about the position of the Muslims in your society. There is a vast difference between the position of the Muslim community in Egypt and that of the Muslim immigrants from North Africa working in Europe. An appreciation of these *sociological factors* can help us to understand how our Muslim neighbours feel about themselves.

3. Find out all you can about the *historical and political factors* which have affected the Muslim communities in your country:

eg
- How has the creation of Pakistan affected the Muslims of Pakistan and India?
- What has been the effect of the conflict between Christian and Muslim communities in Lebanon and in the Philippines?
- How has the creation of the state of Israel affected the Arab world?
- How has Arab control of much of the world's oil resources affected attitudes towards the Arab world?

FOR FURTHER STUDY

1. **Rooting Out Racial and Religious Prejudice** (*Read* Acts 10.1-48)

Q.
- What were the prejudices in Peter's mind which made it difficult for him to meet these Gentiles?
- Do we have similar prejudices which make it hard for us to have close friendships with Muslims, or to believe that Muslims can come to faith in Christ?
- How did the Holy Spirit deal with Peter's prejudices? How can he deal with our prejudices?

2. **The Command to Cross Barriers of Prejudice** (*Read* Acts 1.7-8)

Q. - Why did Jesus mention Samaria by name in this context? (cf Matthew 10.5-6).

3. **The Healing of the Rift Between the Jews and the Samaritans** (*Read* Acts 8.4-17)

Q. - What was the reason for this special apostolic delegation sent from Jerusalem (v.14)?

- What was special and unique about the way in which the Holy Spirit came upon these believers (vv. 15-17)?
- Is there any connection between the circumstances of this visit and the special way in which the Spirit was given on this occasion?
- How would these events have contributed to the healing of the rift between these two communities within the church?

3

THE MUSLIM AT PRAYER

One way of understanding the Muslim is to try to enter sympathetically into what he is doing when he prays. Thus, before studying what he believes (Study 4), we should find out how he prays. Instead of looking on critically as spectators, we should try to appreciate what he is doing and saying, and identify with him as much as we can.

We therefore need to study both THE CALL TO PRAYER and THE FATIHAH.

THE CALL TO PRAYER

(chanted five times a day with variations from every mosque throughout the Islamic World)

> "God is most great, God is most great, I bear witness that there is no god except God: I bear witness that Muhammad is the Apostle of God. Come ye unto prayer. Come ye unto good. Prayer is a better thing than sleep. Come ye to the best deed. God is most great. God is most great. There is no god except God."
>
> (Kenneth Cragg, *The Call of the Minaret,* p. 30)

Q. – Is there any way in which *we* can hear this as a Call to Prayer, and pray *with* and *for* Muslims whenever we hear it?

THE FATIHAH

(the first surah of the Qur'an, recited as part of the prayers five times a day)

"In the Name of the merciful Lord of mercy.
Praise be to God, the Lord of all being,
The merciful Lord of mercy,
Master of the Day of Judgement.

Thee alone we worship
And to Thee alone we come for aid.
Guide us in the straight path,
The path of those whom Thou hast blessed,
Not of those against whom there is displeasure,
Nor of those who go astray."

(Kenneth Cragg, *The Event of the Qur'an,* p.74)

In observing the postures which the Muslim adopts for his ritual prayer, remember:

- that Muhammad may well have learned these postures from Syrian Christian monks;
- that prostration is found in the Bible (eg, Ezekiel 1.28);
- that the Muslim is trying to express his total submission to God in a physical way;
- that Muhammad first taught Muslims to pray towards Jerusalem like the Jews. It was only when his message was rejected by the Jews that they changed the direction to Mecca in accordance with a Qur'anic revelation.

Q. - Can we as Christians share this prayer? Are there any sentiments which we would *not* want to express in prayer?

- Compare the *Fatihāh* with the Lord's Prayer. What are the main similarities and the main differences between the two prayers?
- The Arabic word for this kind of formal prayer is *salāt,* and needs to be distinguished from *du'ā* which means prayers of personal petition. How can we explain to the Muslim the difference between *salāt* and *du'ā* in Christian prayer?

FOR ACTION

1. If you live in a Muslim community and hear the Prayer Call chanted five times a day from the minaret, ask a Muslim to help you to recognise and understand at least some of the Arabic words.

eg, *allahu akbar*	"God is most great"
la illaha ill-allah	"there is no god except God"
hayya li-ssala	"come to prayer"

2. Ask a Muslim to explain to you his *salāt,* the formal prayers which he prays five times a day.

Ask him to explain what prayer means to him and what are the different kinds of prayer which can be offered: the formal prayers (*salāt*) and informal, personal prayer (*du'ā*). You must be careful, however, to avoid any possible misunderstandings, since if you show too much interest in *"salāt",* he may think that you want to become a Muslim!

3. Find a Muslim Prayer Manual which gives the words of the ritual prayers with a translation.

4. If you know a Muslim well enough, ask if you can pray *with him,* and offer a prayer to God about any special needs you or he may have. Ask your Muslim friend to suggest what posture you should adopt for prayer – standing, kneeling or sitting.

The following is an example of a prayer prepared by an Indian Christian for use in the home of a sick Muslim friend:

"O God, creator of the universe – You who created and now sustain all your creation with the word of Your power; we worship You. We remember how great You are and yet how loving You are. There is no one like You. We remember too that You are closer to us than our jugular vein. You know all things and so we are assured that You know each of us – our sin and our sickness. We thank You that You are able to deal with our sinfulness and to heal our diseases. We remember the words that You spoke through Your Prophet Isaiah that all we like sheep have gone astray but You have laid our sins upon Him: even Jesus, and by His being punished we are healed. Look in mercy upon this my friend who is ill and according to Your will and for Your glory heal him of his sickness and cleanse him from his sinful ways. We pray this in the name of Jesus the Messiah. Amen."

(quoted by Vivienne Stacey in *Practical Lessons for Evangelism Among Muslims* (2)

5. Find out what role the mosque plays in the life of your Muslim neighbours:

eg – How many attend the Friday prayers?
- How many pray there at other times?
- Is the mosque a social centre for the community or solely a place of prayer?
- Do women go to the mosque? If not, why not?

6. **Discuss the following Case Study:**

The Muslim community in an inner city area wants to buy an old church building, which has not been used for many years, and turn it into a mosque. The Christian community, however, is very divided over the issue. Some argue that it would be better for the church building to be used as a place of prayer by Muslims than to be demolished or turned into a warehouse. Others believe that it would be dishonouring to the name of Christ for a building which has once been used for Christian worship to be used for Muslim worship.

After discussing some of the issues involved, do the following Role-Play: Imagine that your group is a special committee of the local Council of Churches. Ask different members of the group to express the different points of view, and ask one person to write a brief report clearly setting out some of the issues, so that members of the local churches can make up their minds over the question.

FOR FURTHER STUDY

1. **The Prayers of Other Men** (*Read* Acts 10.1-6)

Q. – Cornelius needed to hear the proclamation of the gospel before he believed. But if God could speak in this way about the prayers of Cornelius even *before* he believed the gospel, how should this affect our thinking about the prayers of the devout Muslim?

2. **The Danger of Judging the Devotion of Others** (*Read* Genesis 20.1-18)

Q. – Abraham seriously misjudged Abimelech and his relationship with God. How can we be guilty of making the same mistake about Muslims and their relationship with God?

3. **Verses about prayer in the Qur'an**

the command to pray	2.43-46
times for prayers	17.78-79
prayers to be said facing Mecca	2.149-150
purification before prayer	5.6
the Friday prayers	62.9-10
circumstances when one is excused from prayer	4.101-103
the value of prayer	29.45

4

BASIC MUSLIM BELIEFS AND PRACTICES

In this study we consider THE ARTICLES OF FAITH, the basic "Creed" of Islam, and THE PRACTICE OF ISLAM, the basic essentials of the practice of Islam.

THE ARTICLES OF FAITH *(imān)* (*Read* Surah 2.285)

"The messenger believeth in that which hath been revealed unto him from His Lord and (so do) the believers. Each one believeth in Allah and His Angels and His scriptures and His messengers. . . ."

According to tradition, Muhammad summarised the basic articles, which a Muslim must believe, as follows: "God, and His Angels, and His Books, and His Apostles; the Last Day, and the Decree of both good and evil."

1. **God:** He is One; his nature and qualities are chiefly revealed in his 99 "Most Beautiful Names".

2. **His Angels:** these include four archangels (eg, Gabriel) and an indefinite number of ordinary angels. There are also creatures between angels and men called *jinn,* some of which are good and some evil.

3. **His Books:** Scriptures were revealed to Adam, Seth, Enoch and Abraham, but these have now been lost. These are the main Scriptures:
   a. The Pentateuch *(tawrāt)*
   b. The Psalms *(zabūr)*
   (both of these are said by Muslims to have been corrupted or misinterpreted by the Jews).
   c. The Gospel *(Injīl)*
   (said by Muslims to have been corrupted or misinterpreted by

the Christians).

4. **His Apostles:** The Qur'an names 28 Apostles, most of whom are biblical characters. The six greatest are Adam, Noah, Abraham, Moses, 'Isa (Jesus) and Muhammad.

5. **The Last Day:** the Day of Judgement, when all men will be judged according to their deeds, and admitted to Paradise or to Hell.

6. **God's Decrees:** ie, God's predestination of everything—both good and evil.
"Fatalism remains very strong at a popular level in the Muslim world, but it is important to note that the Qur'an with its preaching of God's justice rejects the idea of a capricious fate, and that orthodox theology also defends the idea of human responsibility."
(John B. Taylor, *Introducing Islam,* p. 37)

NOTE: There are two main *sources of authority* for what a Muslim believes:

1. The Qur'an itself.

2. The Practice of the Prophet Muhammad (ie, the *sunnah*) as recorded in the Traditions (*hadīth*) which were collected and sifted by biographers and jurists during the 300 years after Muhammad's death.

There are two important *principles of interpretation* which can be appealed to in any discussion about Muslim belief or practice:

1. The Principle of "*Consensus*" (*ijmā'*) which means that since "the community will not agree in an error", one can appeal to what has been the belief and practice of the whole Muslim community.

2. The Principle of "*Analogy*" (*qiyās*) which means that difficult questions can be decided by reference to any previous comparable precedent, especially if it is found in the life of the Prophet himself.

THE PRACTICE OF ISLAM *(dīn)*

The basic essentials in the practice of Islam are summed up in the "Five Pillars":

1. **Recital of the Creed** *(shahāda):* "There is no god but God, and Muhammad is the Apostle of God." Reciting this creed with sincerity qualifies a person to be called a Muslim. It is repeated in every act of ritual worship.

2. **Prayer** *(salāt):* the recital of the ritual prayers five times a day, with the prescribed postures. Friday is a special day of prayer. (*Read* Surah 17:78-79)

3. **Almsgiving** *(zakāt):* the legal alms to be given away, amounting to 1/40th of one's earnings. (*Read* Surah 2:271-273)

4. **Fasting** *(saum):* prescribed during the month of Ramadan for all except the sick, travellers, pregnant women, nursing mothers and young children. The fasting is between first light in the morning until sunset. (*Read* Surah 2:183-187)

5. **Pilgrimage** *(hajj):* all Muslims who are able to are required to make the pilgrimage to Mecca once in their lifetime. The *ka'bah* in Mecca is a sacred shrine because Muslims believe that it was built by Adam, and later rebuilt by Abraham and Ishmael after the Flood. (*Read* Surah 2:196-197)

FOR ACTION

Find out from a Muslim friend whether the following outline of Muslim beliefs is accurate, and gives a fair summary of what most Muslims believe.

Would you agree that what is written in the column on the right is a fair summary of what most Christians believe? Would you want to express your belief differently?

MUSLIM BELIEF	CHRISTIAN BELIEF
REVELATION AND INSPIRATION	
The very words of the Qur'an were revealed to Muhammad. (Surah 12.2-3) Muhammad did not write the Qur'an, he simply received it and recited it, so that his own thoughts and ideas did not contribute to the revelations. (7.157 and 29.48)	The writers of the Bible were inspired by the Holy Spirit. "Men spoke from God" (2 Peter 1.21). The Bible is therefore *both* the word of God *and* the word of men. The writers were not passive instruments used by God like typewriters; they thought about what they were doing and wrote in their own individual style.
It is unnecessary and wrong to try to find the "sources" of the Qur'an.	Although they were inspired, there is no reason why we should not study the Bible as we study other literature and ask questions about the sources, etc.
Because the Qur'an was revealed in Arabic, it is vital to read and recite it in Arabic. Translations of the Qur'an may or may not be permitted; but even when permitted, they do not convey the full meaning of the original.	The OT was written mostly in Hebrew, and the NT writers wrote in Greek and used Greek translations of the OT. We encourage translations of the Bible because we believe God wants all men to understand as best they can. A translation of the Bible is just as much "the Bible" as the original Hebrew and Greek. The meaning of the original *can* be conveyed adequately in any language.
THE TRANSCENDENCE AND SOVEREIGNTY OF GOD	
"God is greater" – eg, he is greater than all our ideas of him. He is the "Lord of all worlds", the Creator and Sustainer of the universe (3.189). At	Christians have a similar belief about the sovereignty of God, but tend to put more emphasis on the nearness of God to man, and speak of God in

the same time he is nearer to man "than the jugular vein" (50.16).

more personal terms.

God is almighty and predestinates everything in the universe, including both good and evil. At the same time man is still held responsible for his actions (4.79).

Christians also try to maintain a balance between God's predestination and man's freedom and responsibility; but we tend to put less emphasis than the Muslim on God's predestination of everything, and never speak of God decreeing or creating evil.

MAN THE CREATURE

The proper relationship of man to God is that of a servant to his Master. "To be the slave of Allah is the proudest boast of the Muslim, bondage to Allah liberating from all other servitudes" (Pickthall).

Man is a creature created in the "image and likeness of God". This image has been spoiled and marred, but not completely destroyed. God wants men to be his "sons" who know him as "Father".

Man has been created as a steward to look after the world God has made (2.30).

We believe similarly that man was created to subdue the earth (Genesis 1.28).

MAN THE SINNER

When Adam sinned, this did not amount to a "Fall" for the whole human race.

Adam's sin affected the whole human race. "Sin came into the world through one man . . ." (Romans 5.12). "In Adam all die" (1 Corinthians 15.22).

Every man is born sinless, with a clean sheet before God.

Original sin means that we inherit the fallen human nature of our parents, and are born in a state of alienation from God. We are not *guilty* before God because of our parents' sin, but we inherit the tendency to sin.

THE LAW OF GOD

God's requirements for man are contained in the law *(sharī'a);* and the most important are the Five Pillars.

God's requirements for man are revealed supremely in the Ten Commandments which cover our relationship with God and with our neighbour. This basic law is explained and amplified in the rest of the OT and the teaching of Jesus.

With the following subjects, put down in the column on the right what you think is a fair summary of what most Christians believe. It can be a helpful discipline to articulate what you believe in terms which the Muslim will understand, and which show that you are sensitive to the similarities and differences between Muslim and Christian beliefs.

FORGIVENESS

God is merciful and willing to forgive all men who sincerely repent, believe and devote themselves to good works. God forgives simply by pronouncing forgiveness. There is no need for any sacrifice or atonement. Forgiveness depends simply on the mercy of God and his declaration of forgiveness (4.106).

SALVATION, HEAVEN AND HELL

Our good deeds and our bad deeds will be weighed in the balance by God on the Day of Judgement. We can trust that, if we live a good life, our good deeds will outweigh our bad deeds; but we cannot know until the Day itself (2.82).

(Some Muslims believe we can trust the intercession of the Prophet to help us.)

If God accepts us, we will be admitted to Paradise; if not, we go to Hell (7.40-46).

(Some Muslims are more universalist and believe that God's mercy will reach to all.)

JESUS

He was a prophet sent by God to the Jews. He was one of the greatest prophets, since he was born of a virgin and worked miracles (5.110).

God rescued him from death by crucifixion, and raised him to heaven (4.156-158).

He will return to earth again before the Day of Judgement.

THE ONENESS OF GOD

God is One, not three – he cannot possibly have a "son" (112.1-4).

Idolatry (*shirk*) means putting anything (a human being, an angel or any other "god") on the same level as God, or associating them with God in any way (7.191-194).

THE PATTERN FOR OUR LIVES

Apart from what is prescribed in the *shari'a* (law), the life and teaching of Muhammad as revealed in the Qur'an and the Traditions give us a pattern of the good life and a standard of the way we should live as individuals and as a community.

(Some Muslims believe that Muhammad was sinless and even pre-existent, though this is not supported by the Qur'an.)

FOR FURTHER STUDY

If you were asked to summarise the main articles of the Christian *faith* under six main headings, how would you do it? What are the six most basic things that you believe?

This may at first seem an impossible or unreasonable task! But if you can summarise simply and clearly what you believe, it may help you to communicate what you believe to a Muslim.

If, when you have done this, you feel that such an outline doesn't convey all that you believe, and doesn't communicate anything about Christian experience or what it feels like to be a Christian, this should help you to appreciate the limitations which a devout Muslim sees in any short summary of Muslim beliefs and practices.

Similarly, if you were asked to explain what are the five Pillars of Christianity, what would you say? What do you think are the five most important things about the *practice* of Christianity?

5

MUHAMMAD

In order to appreciate the life and teaching of Muhammad, we need to know something of the context in which he lived, and the state of Christianity at the time; we also need to understand how his message was related to the main events of his life, and how Islam spread after his death.

We therefore consider these points under the following four headings: ARABIA BEFORE THE TIME OF MUHAMMAD; CHRISTIANITY AT THE TIME OF MUHAMMAD; THE LIFE OF MUHAMMAD; THE SPREAD OF ISLAM AFTER MUHAMMAD.

ARABIA BEFORE THE TIME OF MUHAMMAD

(The "Age of Ignorance", *il jāhiliyyah*)

1. *POLITICAL*

Some of the tribes were nomadic bedouin of the desert; others were semi-nomadic, while others were permanently settled in smaller towns (like Tā'if) or larger cities (like Mecca and Medina). While individual tribes were united by alliances, there was no unity in the area as a whole. Blood-feuds between tribes were settled by the tribal ethic of revenge and reprisal.

2. *FOREIGN POWERS*

The two great World Powers in Muhammad's time were the Byzantine Empire and the Persian Empire; Arabia was influenced by the power struggle between these two great powers. (See map on following page.)

a. **Byzantine Empire** (Asia Minor, Syria, Egypt, SE Europe; capital in Constantinople). Fiercely "Orthodox" (Christian) in doctrine, and

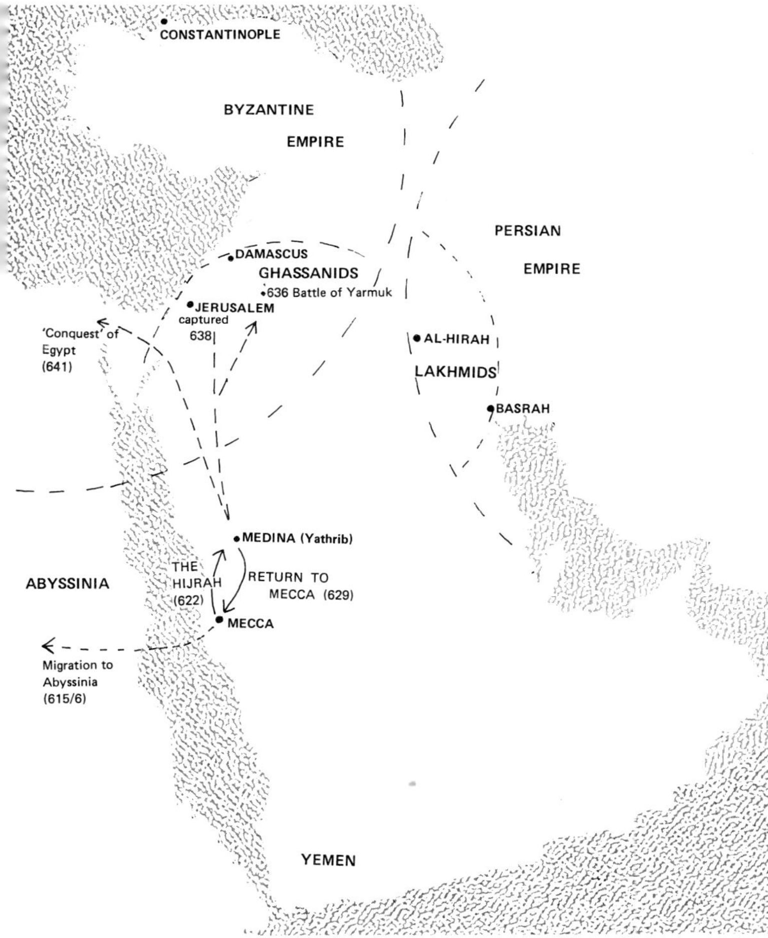
CONSTANTINOPLE
BYZANTINE
EMPIRE
PERSIAN
EMPIRE
DAMASCUS
GHASSANIDS
636 Battle of Yarmuk
JERUSALEM
captured
638
'Conquest' of
Egypt
(641)
AL-HIRAH
LAKHMIDS
BASRAH
MEDINA (Yathrib)
THE
HIJRAH
(622)
RETURN TO
MECCA (629)
ABYSSINIA
MECCA
Migration to
Abyssinia
(615/6)
YEMEN

strongly opposed to other "heretical" doctrines like Monophysitism and Nestorianism.

Supported the Ghassanid Dynasty in Syria as a buffer state against the Arabs.

b. **Persian Empire** under the Sassanid Dynasty (Iraq to Afghanistan; capital in Iraq).

Supported the Lakhmid Kingdom of Hira in Iraq as a buffer against the Arabs.

In 614AD the Persians captured Jerusalem from Byzantine power; but in 628 the Byzantines defeated the Persians. Both empires were exhausted by the struggles, leaving a power vacuum at the time when Islam was beginning to spread.

3. *ECONOMIC AND SOCIAL*

There was a flourishing caravan trade along routes running north-south and east-west. Mecca had become an important commercial centre, as well as a centre of pilgrimage. There were many social evils – eg, female infants were often buried alive, and women had little protection.

4. *RELIGION*

Although there is some evidence of belief in one supreme God (Allah), religious practices centred round a host of lesser deities: eg, at Mecca three goddesses were worshipped: Manat, Al lat, and Al Uzza. There were also many idol cults, and sacrifices were offered to spirits (eg, of caves, trees, wells, stones). Superstitious rituals were practised at many shrines, and there were annual pilgrimages to the major shrines like the Ka'bah at Mecca. There was a strong belief in Fate, and little or no belief in an after-life. A rich tradition of Arab poetry had been developed.

5. *OTHER RELIGIONS*

a. There were some *Jewish* communities or tribes, especially in and around Medina.

b. There were people called *hanīf,* who were a kind of monotheist, but had little influence.

c. *Christians:* There were several nomadic tribes in the Hajaz (around Mecca) which had previously embraced Christianity. The area of Yemen in the south had been Christian since the 4th century.

In Mecca itself the Christians were mostly foreigners – eg, black slaves from Ethiopia, labourers and traders from Syria. According to tradition, Muhammad's first wife Khadijah had a cousin, Waraqah ibn Naufal, who had become a Christian.

Muhammad may well have had some contact with Syrian monks in the desert.

CHRISTIANITY AT THE TIME OF MUHAMMAD

1. The Christianity which Muhammad saw was basically *a foreign religion.* Most of the Christians with whom he came in contact were not Arabs but foreigners from the neighbouring countries, many of whom had settled in Arabia because they had been persecuted elsewhere. They kept themselves aloof from the Arabs; they continued to worship in their own foreign languages. It is generally agreed that Muhammad cannot have had access to any books of the Bible in his own language of Arabic.

2. The Christian Church was *deeply divided over doctrinal disputes.* Ever since the great Councils of Nicaea (AD325) and Chalcedon (451), the churches in the East had been arguing about the doctrines of the Trinity and the person of Christ. Apart from those who accepted the doctrines of Chalcedon, the

- Monophysites emphasised the divinity of Jesus, and gave the impression that Jesus was not fully human;
- Nestorians could not accept that manhood and godhead could be combined in the person of Jesus;
- Gnostics tended to think that matter was evil and that salvation depended on an experience of mystical enlightenment. They denied the incarnation, and some believed that Jesus was not crucified.

3. Christianity was a religion *associated with political power and colonial expansionism.* The Byzantine Emperors stood firmly for the Orthodox faith and fiercely persecuted the different heretical sects. For many Arabs, therefore, Christianity was synonymous with Byzantine domination and fierce repression of any beliefs which differed from the religion of the state.

THE LIFE OF MUHAMMAD

AD c570	Birth of Muhammad; belonged to tribe of Qureish. Father died before he was born, and mother died 6 years later.

	Brought up by grandfather and uncle, Abu Tālib.
c592	According to tradition began travelling to Syria with trading caravans, and on one of these journeys met Bahira, a Syrian Christian monk.
595	Married Khadijah, a wealthy widow, and began working with her in her trading business.
610	Muhammad's first call to be a Prophet, while meditating in a cave on Mt Hira near Mecca.
615/6	Persecution from his own tribe of Qureish forced some of his followers to emigrate to the Christian kingdom of Abyssinia. Muhammad and his "Companions" stayed in Mecca.
619	Death of Khadijah, and of Abu Tālib, Muhammad's uncle and protector. Muhammad's position now less secure in the tribe.
622	*The Emigration (hijrah)* to Medina in response to an invitation from a group of Muslim converts ("Helpers") for him to come to resolve the conflicts between the different communities in Medina. Beginning of the Muslim era.
624	Muslims began raiding caravans from Mecca – which led to a series of battles: Battle of *Badr* – Muslims (with 324 men) defeated Meccans (with 950 men).
625	Battle of *Uhud* – Muslims defeated by Meccans.
627	Battle of *Ahjab* – Muslims repelled the Meccan attack on Medina.
628	The Treaty of Hudaibiyah between Muhammad and the Meccans, which enabled him to return to Mecca for pilgrimage the following year.
629	*Muhammad and the Muslims returned to Mecca* on 11 January with 10,000 men. Meccans submitted without fighting. Muhammad declared a general amnesty. All idols in the *ka'bah* destroyed. Muhammad returned to Medina. Beginning of mass movement of tribes embracing Islam.

631	Muhammad's last Pilgrimage to Mecca.
632	Muhammad died in Medina.

THE SPREAD OF ISLAM AFTER MUHAMMAD

632-634	1st Caliph, Abu Bakr: prevented many tribes from breaking away from the new Islamic state. Defeated Byzantine army in 634.
634-644	2nd Caliph, 'Umar: carried out the collection of the surahs of the Qur'an. Defeated Byzantine army at Battle of Yarmuk (636): captured Jerusalem, and gained control of Syria, Egypt and Persia.
644-656	3rd Caliph, 'Uthman: established official text of the Qur'an and had other texts destroyed.
656-661	4th Caliph, 'Ali, Muhammad's cousin and son-in-law.
660-750	Omayyad Dynasty ruled in Damascus. Golden Age of Islam.
by 732	(100 years after Muhammad's death) Islamic Empire stretched from Spain to Persia.
750-1258	Abassid Dynasty ruled in Baghdad.

NB. 1. In several cases Christians welcomed the spread of Islamic rule; eg, in Syria because it brought relief from Byzantine rule, and in Egypt because the Copts were able to depose a puppet patriarch and recall their own exiled patriarch. The Copts joined forces with the Muslims to drive out the Byzantines.

2. Everyone under Islamic rule paid land tax. Christians and Jews paid in addition a poll tax (*jizyah*), but did not have to do military service or pay the Muslims' alms tax.

3. About the spread of Islam. It is dangerous oversimplification to say that Islam was "spread by the sword".

> "When Islam spread rapidly over much of the civilized world it spread first as a military and political success story; yet it was sometimes centuries before the inhabitants of the conquered lands voluntarily became Muslims. On the other hand, the motive in the minds of the caliphs behind the military and political expansion was that ultimately there should be those conversions to Islam; in the minds of the soldiers, as in every other generation, there was the desire for the spoils of war; but the Muslim

conquests were remarkable for their discipline and lack of wanton destruction." (John B. Taylor, *Introducing Islam,* p 33)

FOR ACTION

Look up some of the passages from the Qur'an noted in the following Study (No. 6, pp 33-36).

FOR FURTHER STUDY

What are we to think of Muhammad as a person?

a. *HIS CHARACTER*

The following are some of the qualities which the earliest traditions attributed to Muhammad: gentleness and tenderness; fondness for children and kindness to animals; courage and resoluteness; impartiality and firmness; wise and clever diplomacy; severity combined with generosity; sincerity, humility and charm.
(Montgomery-Watt, *Muhammad, Prophet and Statesman*, pp 229-231.)

b. *HIS ACHIEVEMENTS*

1. He united the warring factions of Medina and won over the Meccans who had previously opposed him. He united all the tribes of Arabia and made them feel they belonged to one nation, community or federation (*umma*).

2. He gave the Arabs their own scriptures in their own language.

3. He recalled the Arabs to the worship of the One God, and rooted out idolatry and idolatrous practices.

4. He created an Islamic society in which religious authority took the place of tribal authority, and in which law was based on the revealed will of God.

c. *MUHAMMAD AND CHRISTIANITY*

Q. - If the kind of Christianity which Muhammad saw was so imperfect, and if he had no opportunity to read the Bible in Arabic, is it honest and fair to think of Muhammad purely and simply as a "heretic", and to put him into the same category as Arians or Jehovah's Witnesses?

- Is Muhammad to be thought of in terms of Matthew 24.23-25?
- If Muhammad did not have a clear idea of the Trinity or of the Incarnation, how far is it justified to identify him with the "Anti-Christ" in 1 John 2.22-23?

- If the world in which Muhammad lived was more like the world of the Old Testament than of the New Testament, how well does Muhammad stand up to comparison with OT characters like Abraham, Gideon, Solomon, Elijah and David? If we examine their character and their private life (eg, the number of their wives) together with their teaching and their achievements, does Muhammad appear very much better or very much worse than them?

BIBLIOGRAPHY

Montgomery-Watt, *Muhammad, Prophet and Statesman*
David Brown, *The Way of the Prophet*

Muhammad's Relations with Christians

We can trace at least five different stages in the relations between Muhammad (and his immediate followers) and the Christians with whom they came in contact:

1. Muhammad mixed freely with Christians, and learned from them. (*Read* 5.82 and 10.95)

Muslim Tradition asserts that when Muhammad, at an early stage in his ministry, wondered whether or not his revelations came from God, his wife Khadijah encouraged him to consult her cousin, Waraqah ibn Naufal, who was a Christian.

2. Muhammad disputed with Christians, appealing to them to believe that his revelations merely confirmed their scriptures. (*Read* 4.171)

3. Muhammad became more critical of Christians who refused to accept his revelations. (*Read* 5.14 and 5.51)

4. Muhammad sometimes tolerated Christian minorities, which did not become Muslim, but at other times encouraged his followers to fight against all who refused to accept Islam. (*Read* 9.29-30)

5. Abu Bakr, the 1st Caliph (AD632-634), tolerated Christian communities in Arabia which submitted to the political authority of Islam.

It is important to notice that even after Christians had refused to accept Muhammad as a prophet, there were many periods when they were tolerated. The best example in this early period is the Christians of Najran.

6. ‘Umar, the 2nd Caliph (634-644), expelled all Christians from Arabia.

Q. - Which of these six stages seems most applicable to the situation in which you find yourself with your Muslim neighbours?

eg - national Christians in Saudi Arabia would say No. 6.

- Christian students mixing freely with educated Muslim students in a western university would say No. 1.
- Christians in countries with a Muslim majority would say No. 5.

6

THE QUR'AN

Most Christians find the Qur'an very difficult to read. We therefore need to ask two basic questions: WHAT DOES THE QUR'AN MEAN TO THE MUSLIM? and HOW SHOULD WE START READING THE QUR'AN?

WHAT DOES THE QUR'AN MEAN TO THE MUSLIM?

1. It is essential to realize that the Qur'an is to the Muslim what Jesus is to the Christian. It is a mistake to make a direct comparison between the role of Jesus in Christianity and the role of Muhammad in Islam, or between the place of the Bible in Christianity and the place of the Qur'an in Islam.

> "Muslims and Christians have been alienated partly by the fact that both have misunderstood each other's faith by trying to fit it into their own pattern. The most usual error is to suppose (on both sides) that the roles of Jesus Christ in Christianity and of Muhammad in Islam are comparable. We suggest that much more insight is gained if one realizes that the role of St Paul in Christianity and that of Muhammad in Islam are much more closely comparable. Both are apostles. St Paul preached a message, as Muhammad did; only his message, and the message of Christianity, is the person of Christ. If one is drawing parallels in terms of the structure of the two religions, what corresponds in the Christian scheme to the Qur'an is not the Bible but the person of Christ – it is Christ who is for Christians the revelation of (from) God."
>
> (Wilfred Cantwell-Smith, *Islam in Modern History,* pp 25-26)

2. Muslims believe that the revelation of the Qur'an was itself a miracle, since Muhammad himself was not able to read or write. This belief is summed up by the Arabic word *i'jāz,* meaning the incomparability of the Qur'an. It is based on verses in the Qur'an like the following:

"Those who follow the messenger, the Prophet who can neither read nor write, whom they will find described in the Torah and the Gospel . . ." (7.157).

"And thou (O Muhammad) wast not a reader of any scripture before it, nor didst thou write it with thy right hand, for then might those have doubted, who follow falsehood" (29.48).

It should be noted, however, that although Muslims have generally understood the word *ummi* to mean "illiterate", a number of scholars have suggested that this was not the original meaning of the word. Pickthall translates it "the Prophet who can neither read nor write", while A. J. Arberry translates it "the Prophet of the common folk", and Kenneth Cragg suggests "the unlettered prophet", in the sense of the "prophet for those who are yet without Scriptures".

3. In order to appreciate what the Qur'an means to the Muslim we ought to hear it recited. Since the Qur'an was revealed in Arabic, the Arabic of the Qur'an is an essential part of the message, and part of the appeal of the Qur'an for the Muslim lies in the beauty of the Arabic. Translating it into other languages is therefore like translating Shakespeare, and a great deal of the quality of the original is lost in translation. In the past translations were generally discouraged, if not actually forbidden. Today, however, they are being allowed, and some have the approval of Muslim leaders, although they are regarded as a kind of paraphrase and have to be given titles like "The Meaning of the Glorious Koran".

4. The Muslim hears the Qur'an as a message which calls him to worship and surrender. He is not worried about the lack of chronology in the Qur'an or by the absence of any sense of historical development. The heading of each surah indicates whether it was revealed at Mecca (ie, between 610 and 622) or at Medina (ie, between 622 and 632), and the Muslim learns how to relate particular passages to incidents in the life of the Prophet.

HOW SHOULD WE START READING THE QUR'AN?

It is probably just as hard for a Christian to read the Qur'an from beginning to end as for a Muslim to read the Bible from Genesis to Revelation! The following, therefore, are some of the points at which we can begin to read it:

Note: The following verse numbers are from Pickthall's translation; in some other translations of the Qur'an the numbering of verses is slightly different. If the verses you have looked up in your translation do not seem to be the right ones, read a few verses *before* or *after,* until you find the right verses.

1. *THE SHORTEST SURAHS*

Surah 1 – The Fātihah, often described as "the essence of the Qur'an".

96 – said to be the first surah revealed to Mohammad.

74 – said to be the second surah revealed after some months.

82, 84, 93, 101, 112, 113, 114
– all short surahs at the end of the Qur'an.

2. *SOME WELL KNOWN PASSAGES*

2.255 – a well known verse about the sovereignty of God.

24.35-36 – a passage which has been a source of inspiration to mystics.

2.256 – "there is no compulsion in religion".

59.22-24 – verses about "the most beautiful names" of God.

3. *TYPICAL PASSAGES*

- about the Creation, 3.189-191; 13.2-4; 31.10-11; 32.4-9.
- about heaven and hell, 2.24-25; 38.49-60; 44.47-57.
- about prophets, 2.124-134.

4. *LAWS*

– about marriage, 4.3.
theft, 5.38.
usury, 2.275-279.
obedience to parents, 29.8.
wine, 2.219.
pork, 2.173.

- a summary of the moral law, 2.83; 2.177.

5. *USE THE INDEX* to look up subjects like: Abraham, Marriage, Divorce, Jews, Christians, Satan, Adultery, etc.

6. *COMPLETE SURAHS*

12 Joseph (compare and contrast with the story of Joseph in Genesis, chapters 37-50).

2 The Cow – generally said to be the first surah revealed at Medina; one of the longer surahs, but one which contains many important Quranic themes.

FOR ACTION

Look up the following verses in the Qur'an:

1. *ABOUT THE QUR'AN ITSELF*

   The Qur'an revealed in the Arabic language, 12.2; 46.12.
   Muhammad "the seal of the prophets", 33.40.
   The Qur'an reveals clearly what Jews and Christians have hidden in their scriptures, 5.15.
   Verses about "Abrogation", the belief that some revelations to the Prophet can be superseded by later revelations, 2.106; 16.101; 22.52.

2. *ABOUT THE BIBLE*

   - revelations in scripture recognized by the Qur'an:
     - the *tawrāt* (revealed to Moses), 2.87; 3.3.
     - the *zabūr* (revealed to David), 4.163.
     - the *injīl* (revealed to Jesus), 5.46-48.
   - the Qur'an confirms the message of previous scriptures: 2.91; 3.1-4; 3.84; 4.47.
   - God has protected the scriptures: 5.48; 18.28.
   - Muhammad is to consult the scriptures already revealed if he is in doubt about what is revealed to him: 10.94-95.
   - Jews and Christians are accused of tampering with their scriptures:

   a. they are ignorant of them, 2.78.
   b. they conceal them, 2.146, 159, 174; 5.15.
   c. they change them, 2.75.
   d. they sell false scriptures for gain, 2.79.
   e. they believe parts and disbelieve other parts, 2.85.

3. *ABOUT CHRISTIANS*

   a. passages which are *sympathetic:* 2.62, 136-137; 5.69, 82; 22.40.
   b. *appeals to Christians to accept Muhammad's message* because it confirms the *injīl,* 3.64-71; 29.46.
   c. passages which are more *critical:* 5.14; 5.51; 9.29-31; 57.27.

4. *PASSAGES ABOUT JESUS*

   a. the annunciation, and the birth of Jesus, 3.35-47; 19.16-35.
   b. the ministry of Jesus, 3.48-54; 5.110-117; 57.27; 61.6.
   c. the death of Jesus, 3.55; 19.33; 5.117; 4.155-159.
   d. Jesus and God, 3.59; 4.171-172; 5.72-75, 116-117; 9.30-31.

PART 2

7

MUSLIMS AND ISLAM

The aim of this study is to help us to appreciate the differences between Muslims, and to appreciate each Muslim as an individual.

Studies of this kind have many limitations, and can even have certain dangers:

- if they make us think that all Muslims are alike, we need to notice

a. *UNITY AND DIVERSITY IN ISLAM;*

- if they make us think only of the theory of Islam, at its very best, we may need to consider

b. *IDEALS AND REALITIES IN ISLAM;*

- if they concentrate on Islam purely as a system of theological beliefs, we need to be reminded of the place of

c. *HEAD AND HEART IN ISLAM.*

UNITY AND DIVERSITY IN ISLAM

The Muslim believes that there is much more unity among Muslims than there is among Christians. One of the reasons for this unity has been the authority and unanimity of orthodox theologians and jurists over the centuries. At the same time, however, there are many significant differences between the different branches of Islam and the different movements within Islam.

The Two Main Branches of Islam

The break between the two branches goes back to AD661 – the year that Ali, the 4th Caliph, died.

THE SUNNIS ("Orthodox" Muslims)	THE SHI'IS ("Sectarian" Muslims)
The Sunnis accepted all the first four caliphs and accepted the claims of the Umayyad Dynasty in Damascus to take over the caliphate.	The Shi'ites accepted the 4th Caliph, Ali, but did not accept the first three because they believed the line of succession from Muhammad should have been through Ali, the son-in-law of Muhammad. Therefore they wanted Ali's two sons Hasan and Husayn to succeed to the caliphate; but Hasan renounced his claim and Husayn was killed at the Battle of Kerbala in AD680. This martyrdom is very important for Shi'ite Muslims, and is re-enacted annually. It means that Shi'is have some idea of redemptive suffering.
There were Sunni caliphs from 7th century until the end of the Abassid caliphate in 1258. The Ottomans revived the caliphate in 1775; but it was finally abolished in 1924.	Rival *imams* led the Shi'ite community until the 12th, who disappeared in 874. It is believed that he and his successors have been in hiding ever since, waiting until the time for restoration. They have their own secret books of the interpretation of the Qur'an.
Found all over the Islamic World.	Found mostly in Iran, Iraq and Lebanon.

W. Montgomery Watt sums up the essential difference between Shi'i and Sunni Islam in the following way:

> "The essence of Shi'ism is belief in the imam or charismatic leader, which includes the belief that salvation, or keeping to the straight path and avoiding error, comes from following the imam, in contrast to the Sunnite belief that it comes from being a member of the charismatic community. In keeping with the essential belief, the imam came to be regarded as a source of truth or guidance for his followers."

(*Muslim Intellectual, A Study of al-Ghazāli,* Edinburgh University Press, 1963, p 80)

Movements within Islam

a. *THE JURISTS:* Four main schools of interpretation of the Islamic *shari'a* (law), each giving a different emphasis to the different principles of interpretation. They are Hanafi; Shafi'i; Maliki; and Hanbali (most conservative).

b. *THE THEOLOGIANS:*

eg, al-Ash'ari (d.935) – founder of the main school of orthodox theology.

al-Ghazāli (d.1111) – the great philosopher-theologian who was deeply influenced by the Sufis.

c. *THE PHILOSOPHERS:*

eg, The Mu'tazilites (8th and 9th centuries) – philosophical theologians who attempted to give a rational interpretation of basic beliefs.

al-Razi (d.925) – tried to place reason alongside revelation,

al-Farabi (d.950) – tried to explain revelation in rational terms,

ibn Sina (d.1037) = Avicenna – revelation needs to be added to reason.

d. *THE MYSTICS (THE SUFIS)*

The Mystical Movement within Islam began in the 8th and 9th centuries, partly as a call to return to a simple ascetic life with devotional practices (eg, the dervish rituals using the name of God), and partly as a reaction against the excesses of the jurists, the theologians and the philosophers. They developed many Sufi orders (similar to Christian orders or communities), which kept Islam very much alive among the people and became a strong missionary movement. Two well known Sufis are:

al-Junayd (d.908) – emphasized the idea of union with God.

al-Hallāj (d.922) – went further in his ideas of union with God, and claimed "I am the truth". Crucified as a heretic.

e. *OTHER MOVEMENTS AND COMMUNITIES*

Isma'ilis are a branch of the Shi'is, named after Isma'il, the 7th Imam. Present head – the Agha Khan.

Wahabism is a fundamentalist form of Islam, especially strong in Saudi Arabia.

The Muslim Brotherhood (Arab World) and the **Jama'at-i-Islami** (Pakistan): conservative movements which aim at turning Islamic countries into full Islamic states based on Islamic law (the *shari'a*).

The Ahmadiyyah Movement started in the Punjab in 1879 by Ghulam Ahmad Mirza, and became a strong missionary force. In 1974 it was declared by the Pakistan government to be a non-Muslim community, because it recognizes its founder as a prophet who came after Muhammad.

Q. - Which branch of Islam do most of our Muslim neighbours belong to?

- How strong is the influence of different movements on the Muslim Community - eg, the Muslim Brotherhood, Sufism?

IDEALS AND REALITIES IN ISLAM

Throughout these studies we have been trying to appreciate Islam at its very best. It is unfair and dishonest to compare the *best* of what we know and experience in Christianity with the *worst* that we see in Islam. If we concentrate on the worst features of Islam in any situation, we cannot protest when the Muslim speaks about the worst features of the Christianity he knows.

One way of appreciating the best in Islam is to ask what is the secret of the strong appeal of Islam in the world today. The following are some of the answers which may be suggested:

1. It is a simple monotheistic creed without complicated dogmas and without the schisms of Christianity.
2. It is an international brotherhood with a strong sense of community which cuts across differences of race, colour and caste. This sense of community is demonstrated in the Pilgrimage.
3. It appeals to the oppressed - especially in the Third World, because it is concerned with the establishment of a just society.
4. It offers clear guidance about how to live, and claims to be relevant to all the problems of the 20th century - social, economic and political, etc.
5. It presents itself as an alternative to the materialism and atheism of Communism and to the decadence of the so-called "Christian" west.
6. It meets the immediate personal needs in Muslims' lives - viz, the need for direction, power, healing and protection, etc.

Q. - Do any of these answers explain why non-Muslims are being attracted to Islam?

- Does Islam in our situation have any appeal to those *outside* the Muslim community?

Assuming that we appreciate what Islam can be at its very best, what if we do not always see Islam at its best? What if we do not find the "pure" Islam of the Qur'an?

The following are some features of Islam in different parts of the Islamic world which are undoubtedly *non-Islamic*. They represent a departure from the Islam of the Qur'an:

1. The veneration of the Prophet Muhammad (found especially in Pakistan).

2. Maraboutism - a system which enables pilgrims to obtain special blessing (*baraka*) from holy men or holy places (found in North Africa).

3. Veneration of saints; visiting tombs of saints, praying to the saints.

4. Pre-Islamic religion - eg, animism, superstition.

5. The influence of western secular thought (eg, in French literature in North Africa and in secular/nominally Muslim novelists in Egypt).

Q. - How pure a form of Islam do we have in our society?
- Are there any non-Islamic elements in the Islam that we see?
- Could the Muslim offer a similar analysis of non-Christian elements in the Christianity that he sees – e.g., in English folk religion, in Mexican rural Catholicism, or political expressions of Christianity in Northern Ireland?

HEAD AND HEART IN ISLAM

A recent study by Bill Musk entitled "*Popular Islam: The Hunger of the Heart*" attempts to understand the gulf between "High" Islam (ie, the official teaching of Islam based on the Qur'an) and "Low" Islam (ie, popular or folk Islam).

Musk quotes two missionaries who worked for many years among Muslims - Samuel Zwemer (1867-1952) who worked in the Arab world and the Rev Detmar Scheunemann who worked in Indonesia.

> "The student of Islam will never understand the common people unless he knows the reasons for their curious beliefs and practices . . . all of which still blind and oppress mind and heart with constant fear of the unseen. Witchcraft, sorcery, spells, and charms are the background of the native Muslim psychology to an extent that is realized only by those who have penetrated most deeply into the life of the people." (Samuel Zwemer)

"Working for many years in a Muslim country, I have come to the conclusion that the power of Islam does not lie in its dogma and practices, nor in the antithesis of the Trinity, against the Lordship of Christ and his redeeming death, but in the occult practices of its leaders, thus holding sway over their people." (Rev Detmar Scheunemann)

Musk urges that instead of concentrating on "pure" Islam, we ought to be aware of how Muslims feel about Islam and how they practise it. Instead of seeing Islam as a set of doctrines which answer the questions of the intellect, we ought to see how in practice Islam is meeting the hunger of the Muslim's heart.

In the following diagram he notes in the column on the left the felt-needs in popular Islam; in the middle column some of the ways in which these needs are met in forms of popular Islam which are

Felt-Needs in Popular Islam	Animistic Answers to Felt-Needs Not acceptable . . . More acceptable			Christian Answer to Felt-Needs
fear of the unknown	idolatry stone worship	fetishes talismans charms	superstition	security in Christ as Guide Keeper
fear of evil	sorcery witchcraft	amulets knots	exorcism (?)	exorcism, protection in Christ
fear of the future	angel worship	divination spells (?)	fatalism fanaticism	trust in Christ as Lord of the future
shame of not being in the group	magic curse or bless	hair/nail trimmings		acceptance in fellowship of believers
powerless of individual against evil	saint worship		baraka saint/angel petitioning	authority and power of the Holy Spirit
meaninglessness of life		familiar spirit (?)		purpose in life as God's child
sickness	tree/saint worship	healing magic (?)		divine healing

(*Popular Islam: the Hunger of the Heart,* Bill A. Musk, in The Gospel and Islam. A 1978 Compendium, Don M. McCurry, MARC (1979) pp 208/221. See also his discussion of the gulf between 'High' Islam and 'Low' Islam in the same article.)

deeply influenced by animism; and in the column on the right he notes how these same felt-needs can be met in the person of Christ.

Q. – "Christ, in his dealings with ordinary people around him, tended to free them from the 'ideal' religion of the professionals. Why educate the ordinary Muslims in their own faith so that Christ can meet them there tomorrow when he can meet them more fundamentally at the point of their felt-needs today?" (Musk)

FOR FURTHER STUDY

The Gospel and Culture

(based on notes prepared by Bill A. Musk)

WHAT DO WE MEAN BY "CULTURE"?

When we talk about "culture", we are talking about something man-made. "Culture is a *way of life;* culture is the *total plan* for living; it is functionally organized into a *system*; it is *acquired through learning*; it is the way of life of a *social group*, not of an individual as such" (Luzbetak).

The "world-view" of a society is that inner, often inferred, corpus of attitudes or motivations which provide a society with its own unique genre. It is what makes an Englishman English, or an Arab Arab.

There is no such thing as "*the* Christian world-view" or even "*a* Christian world-view", since a world-view is associated with a particular culture and cannot be detached from it. Every world-view or culture has some elements which come under the judgment of Christ as being sinful, while other elements can be transformed in such a way that the society becomes more truly Christian.

In order to illustrate the differences between cultures, let us take as examples what is loosely called "Western Culture" and "Middle Eastern Culture". At the risk of over-simplification, we can make certain very broad generalisations:

Western Culture tends to be	*Middle Eastern Culture* tends to be
individualistic	family-centred
efficiency-oriented	relationship-oriented
man-centred	God-centred

The following diagrams illustrate some of the different values and customs which these cultures accept as normative:

Family

the nuclear family
old people put in Homes

Social Life

equality of sexes;
time-oriented
relationships - eg,
work, leisure

WESTERN WORLD-VIEW

Education

achievement-oriented;
less emphasis
on rote learning

Religion

individualistic
compartmentalized -
sacred and secular separated

Family

the extended family
old people respected
and kept in family

Social Life

segregation
of sexes;
hospitality -
importance of
relationships

MIDDLE-EASTERN WORLD-VIEW

Education

life-centred;

more emphasis
on rote learning

Religion

communal
religion and culture
are inseparable;
no difference between sacred
and secular

HOW CAN WE BE SENSITIVE TO CULTURAL ISSUES?

The following questions may help us to be more aware of our own culture, to be more critical of it and willing for it to be judged by the Gospel. This in turn may help us to be more sensitive to the culture of our Muslim neighbours, and to leave them to respond to Christ with complete freedom from within their own culture.

Q. - To what extent are our ideas of what constitutes truthfulness determined by Scripture, and to what extent are they the result of social conditioning (eg, "white lies", permissible lying on April Fool's Day)?

- Are our tastes in music determined by what we believe about God and the universe, or by what we have been taught to appreciate?
- Have we any right to say that the nuclear family is nearer to the will of God for society than the extended family, or vice versa?
- How does our world-view differ from the world-view of the Muslims we know?
- Are there any important differences between our way of life and the way of life of our Muslim neighbours and friends - eg, in marriage, social customs, language, etc?

IS THE MUSLIM RESPONDING TO THE GOSPEL AND/OR TO OUR CULTURE?

We need to be aware of what is happening when a Muslim begins to respond to what he sees and hears of the Gospel:

- Our Muslim friend may be attracted by many things in the culture of "the missionary" or of the Christian; he may change some of his ideas while underneath his world-view remains basically the same, unaffected by the transforming message of Christ.

eg, he may like western music, literature, and social customs, but still believe in magic; and his ideas of God and of right and wrong remain the same.

- He may make changes only in his way of life, but not at world-view level:

eg, he may start conforming to behaviour patterns of the Christians he knows, whether they are foreigners or of his own nationality.

- Our Muslim friend may, on the other hand, make a much more complete change of mind, both at world-view level and consequently in his way of life:

eg, he may begin to relate to God as Father;
he may have a different idea of what heaven is like;
he may come to accept different moral standards.

These issues are not purely theoretical. If we are not aware of what *we* are doing when we share the Gospel, and what *the Muslim* is doing when he opens himself to the Gospel, we may make certain serious mistakes:

- We may believe that when the Muslim makes certain statements he has been "converted", when in fact all he has done is to repeat a formula which we wanted him to accept.
- We may believe that his interest in Christianity is an interest in the Gospel, when in fact it is little more than an interest in our culture.
- We may think that the Muslim who is attracted by Christian ideas is accepting Christian beliefs as a whole, when in fact he is simply incorporating particular ideas which appeal to him into what is still fundamentally an Islamic world-view.
- We may think that the Muslim's rejection of Christ is a rejection of the Gospel, when in fact it is merely a rejection of a message which has come in an alien and unfamiliar guise. It may be our culture that he is rejecting rather than the Gospel itself.

8

DISCUSSION WITH MUSLIMS

In this study we deal with three basic questions: HOW CAN WE FIND NATURAL POINTS OF CONTACT? HOW CAN WE TAKE THE INITIATIVE IN DISCUSSION? and HOW SHOULD WE HANDLE CONTROVERSY?

HOW CAN WE FIND NATURAL POINTS OF CONTACT?

As we get to know our Muslim neighbours, we will soon find subjects to talk about which arise out of *their* experience and religious observances. The following are some points of contact noted by Vivienne Stacey, based on her many years of experience in Pakistan:

"1. **Amulets.** Amulets or charms generally contain a paper on which is written a verse from the Qur'an. Christians sometimes declare that the wearing of an amulet is wrong and urge the person to take it off. Surely it would be better to enquire whether the person thinks God prefers His words to be around our necks or in our hearts. We can then share words of God which we have memorized and hidden in our hearts. Psalm 119.11.

2. **The wearing of the veil (burqa).** Women often ask why we do not wear the veil. One answer is to spiritualize the matter and to say, "Yes, I wear a spiritual veil all the time." Of course, we have to give a full explanation. Isaiah 61.10 and Romans 13.14.

3. **The creed.** The Muslim who says so often "There is no God but God and Muhammad is his apostle" will sometimes ask us about his creed and ours. John 17.3 is a useful summary of the Christian creed as it speaks of the One God, of Jesus His Apostle or sent one and of knowing God.

4. **Prayer.** A discussion on prayer can lead us into an explanation of the Lord's Prayer which so many Christians pray every day. Luke 11.2-4.

5. **Fasting.** Especially during the fast of Ramadam Muslims enquire from Christians about their beliefs and practices in regard to fasting. Isaiah 58 is a helpful passage to study and explain.

6. **Almsgiving.** The basis for Christian almsgiving and good works can be discussed. 2 Corinthians 9.15.

7. **Pilgrimage.** John 14.1-6 describe the pilgrim, the pilgrim city and the pilgrim way. Jesus is the way (practice), the truth (belief) and the life (experience).

8. **Other words.** It is not always religious words which are points of contact. During the summer of 1978 a Pakistani fellow traveller on the back of a Land Rover spoke of what Mr Zulfikar Ali Bhutto had done to help the remote Northern regions of Pakistan in which we were travelling. He said that several people had volunteered to die in Bhutto's place. I asked him if he had ever heard of a completely innocent man who long ago was allowed to die in the place of others. This led on to some account of the death of Christ for us.

"In conclusion, let it be said that to be effective communicators we have to understand our Muslim friend's way of thinking. We have to enter into his mind, his heart, his emotions, his shoes."

(*Practical Lessons for Evangelism Among Muslims.*)

Q. – What other natural points of contact can we think of which could lead into discussion with a Muslim?

HOW CAN WE TAKE THE INITIATIVE IN DISCUSSION?

We may sometimes feel we can take the initiative and ask questions like these about the Muslim's understanding and his experience:

- how does God forgive us when we sin? Can you be sure that God has forgiven you? Or do you have to wait until the Day of Judgment?
- what are the things you fear most: sickness, rejection, being possessed by evil spirits, etc. . . .?
- do you say prayers of petition (*du'ā*) in addition to the prescribed prayers (*salāt*)? Do you pray using your own words?
- if God is Almighty, why should we pray? If everything is decreed by God, what is the value of prayer?
- do you believe in Fate? What does it mean to you in your life?

- who do you go to for help in a crisis? For example, what do you do when your baby suddenly falls ill? Who do you go to for help – a doctor? the sheikh, imam, maulvi? the medicine man, the witchdoctor . . .?

HOW SHOULD WE HANDLE CONTROVERSY?

Basic Guidelines

a. Don't start the controversy if you can help it!
   - resist the temptation to quarrel (2 Timothy 2.23-26).
   - resist the temptation to criticize Islam (Matthew 7.1-5).

b. Do all you can to remove misunderstandings
   eg, about Christians worshipping three gods
   about Jesus as the physical Son of God
   about the west being "Christian"
   about what it means to be "a Christian".

c. Distinguish between what is important and what is unimportant:
   eg, don't spend all your time debating secondary issues (like pork and wine) if you cannot deal with the more important subjects as well (like the role of the law, the need of man, forgiveness etc).

d. Be prepared to admit the mistakes and crimes of Christians in the past and present (Romans 2.24, Psalm 106.6).

e. Be positive
   - don't always be defending Christianity or attacking Islam.
   - take every opportunity to say what you believe and why you believe it (1 Peter 3.15).

f. Love is more persuasive than any argument
   - even if you win an argument, you may lose the person; even if you lose an argument, you may still win the person if you show that you really love him.

Christian Belief

The following are some of the main areas in which we are likely to find ourselves in controversy with Muslims:

a. The Bible: "Christians have corrupted the Scriptures".
b. Jesus: "God cannot have a son – this is blasphemous".
c. The cross: "the Qur'an says that Jesus did not die on the cross".
d. The Trinity: "God cannot be 3 and 1; Christians worship 3 gods".

Q. - What is the basis for these Muslim arguments?
   - what is the thinking behind these objections?
   eg, *why* does the Muslim think it was inconceivable that Jesus should be crucified?

why does the Muslim reject the Trinity?

- Are we as Christians partly to blame, because of the misleading way in which we have presented these beliefs?
- What should we be learning from these objections and challenges?
- What kind of information and teaching do we need to help us to find answers to these questions?

eg, what literature is available in our language to help us and to help the Muslim?

See further: The 'Corruption' of the Bible, pp. 52ff.; Jesus 'the Son of God', pp. 77ff.; The Death of Jesus, pp. 81ff.

Practical Issues

The following are some of the practical issues often raised in conversation and discussion:

pork

"The Qur'an forbids pork because it is unclean; why do Christians eat it?"

wine

"The Qur'an forbids alcohol - but it is not forbidden for Christians."

asceticism

"Islam has a much more healthy attitude to the physical pleasures of life; it does not demand an unnatural degree of self-denial."

priesthood

"Islam has no priesthood, no special caste of people set aside to perform priestly functions which no one else can perform."

Israel, Zionism and Christianity

"Many Christians support the state of Israel."

western imperialism

"Christianity has been spread in the east through western imperialism."

decline of religion in the west

"The Christian west is suffering from moral and spiritual decline."

Q. - To what extent are such Muslim criticisms about the practice of Christianity justified?

- What can we learn when we find out how others see us?

What are the deeper issues behind some of these questions?

eg, pork and wine: the role of law, the weakness of human nature:

western imperialism: attitudes to political power.

FOR FURTHER STUDY

Learning to Rethink and Restate our Faith

Paul was an orthodox Jew and had been brought up as a Pharisee (Philippians 3.5). After his conversion he continued to work among Jews wherever he went, but he believed that he had a special call to be "an apostle to the Gentiles" (Galatians 2.8).

What difference did this make to the way he sought to communicate the Gospel? It meant that he was willing to rethink his message and present it in ways which Gentiles would understand. Compare his approach with Jews and his approach with Gentiles:

with Jews	*with Gentiles*
Paul's address to Jews in Antioch is basically a review of the meaning of Israel's history. (Acts 13.14-41)	Paul's brief appeal to a Gentile audience at Lystra concentrates on God the Creator. (Acts 14.14-18)
	Paul's address at the Areopagus in Athens begins with points of contact with his Gentile audience. (Acts 17.16-31)
In speaking to Jews Paul could use expressions like "the kingdom of God" which were taken from the OT and had been used by Jesus. (Acts 14.22)	In speaking to Gentiles. Paul could use a word like "mystery", a word taken from the Greek mystery religions, which would have meant little to the Jew. In its original context it referred to the secret myths and rituals known only to the initiated; but Paul gave it a new meaning in its Christian context. (Ephesians 3.9-10)

Q. - Can Paul's example help us as Christians to know why and how to adapt our presentation of the Gospel to the Muslim?

eg,- are there any ideas or expressions which we should deliberately avoid?

- are there ideas, customs or traditions within Islam which can be used to convey some aspect of the Gospel?

Jesus in Discussion and Controversy with the Jews

Read Mark 7.1-23

Q. - What started the discussion (vv 1-5)?

- What was the main point at issue?
- What important truth was Jesus able to explain (vv 20-23)?
- Are there any principles we can apply in our discussion with Muslims about similar issues?

Read Mark 12.28-34 and John 8.44

Q. - How could Jesus say such totally different things to people who were all devout, orthodox Jews: "you are not far from the kingdom of God" and "you are of your father the Devil"?

- What does this teach us about the danger of generalizations, and the need to appreciate each person as an individual and not as a type?

The "Corruption" of the Bible

How are we to answer the common objection that the text of the Bible has been corrupted?

a. There are only four verses in the Qur'an which speak about "corruption" *(tahrīf),* and they do not imply that the *text* of the Bible has been corrupted:

"Some of those who are Jews *change* the words from their context... distorting with their tongues and slandering religion . . ." (or "pervert words from their meanings" [Bell]) 4.46.

"They *change* words from their context and forget a part of that whereof they were admonished" 5.13.

". . . the Jews: listeners for the sake of falsehood, listeners on behalf of other folk who come not unto thee, *changing* words from their context . . ." 5.41.

". . . a party of them used to listen to the Word of Allah, then used to *change* it, after they had understood it, knowingly" 2.75.

The basic accusation in these verses seems to be that certain Jews deliberately mispronounced words spoken by Muhammad, probably playing on the resemblance between certain Arabic and Hebrew words.

In other verses the Jews are accused of "hiding" or "concealing" their Scriptures:

"a party of them knowingly *conceal* the truth" 2.146 (cf. 2.159, 174).

"O people of the Scripture! Now hath Our Messenger come unto you, expounding unto you much of that which ye used to *hide* in the Scripture . . ." 5.15 (cf. 6.92).

This probably means that in discussion with Muslims the Jews refused to quote verses which would support the teaching of Islam (eg, prophecies which could be interpreted as referring to the coming of Muhammad).

b. The accusation about the corruption of the text of the Bible was developed later by Muslim apologists

Muslim writers from the time of Muhammad to the 11th century consistently understood the Quranic verses about "corruption" to mean that Jews and Christians had *misinterpreted* their Scriptures.

Al-Ghazāli, for example (d.1111), wrote a treatise on the Trinity in which he quoted many passages from the Bible, without ever questioning the trustworthiness of the text.

The accusation that Jews and Christians had tampered with the text of their Scriptures first appeared in the writings of Muslim apologists from the 12th century onwards. It was probably developed to explain the many discrepancies between the Bible and the Qur'an.

c. If Muslims claim that the Gospel of Barnabas is the original *injīl* which was revealed to Jesus, it is not difficult to show from internal evidence (eg, the serious errors in history and geography, and points at which it contradicts the Qur'an), that it was written in the 17th century. The author was probably a Spaniard of Jewish background who had recently converted to Islam. The manuscript was discovered in Amsterdam in 1709.

d. In answering the Muslim who says that our Scriptures have been corrupted, we can politely but firmly ask the following question: *when* were they corrupted and *by whom?*

- If he says they were corrupted *before the time of Muhammad,* we can ask him to explain why the Qur'an says that the message revealed to Muhammad was simply a confirmation of previous Scriptures:

  "He hath revealed unto thee (Muhammad) the Scripture with truth, confirming that which was (revealed) before it, even as He revealed the Torah and the Gospel" 3.3 (cf. 2.136; 4.136; 10.95; 41.43).

It is clear that the Scriptures referred to here must be the Scriptures which the Jews and Christians had in their hands at that time:

"Believe in what We have revealed confirming *that which ye possess"* 4.47 (cf. 2.91).

" . . . the Torah and the Gospel *(which are) with them*" 7.157. Muhammad frequently spoke of God watching over the Scriptures to protect them from being changed:

"And unto thee have We revealed the Scripture with truth, confirming whatever Scripture was before it, and a watcher over it" 5.48 (cf. 6.116; 10.65; 18.28).

How, then, could Muhammad say, on the one hand, "the revelations contained in the Qur'an are simply a confirmation of the Scriptures of the Jews and Christians", and on the other hand claim "the Scriptures which the Jews and Christians have in their hands have been corrupted"?

- If he says they were corrupted *after the time of Muhammad,* we can point out that the manuscripts on which our present Bible is based were written centuries before the time of Muhammad. For example, the Dead Sea Scrolls, which include manuscripts of every book of the Old Testament except one, were written before AD68. One of the oldest Greek manuscripts of the whole of the New Testament, the Codex Alexandrinus, dates from the 5th century AD, and can be seen by anyone in the British Museum in London; and manuscripts of some parts of the New Testament can be dated to the 2nd century AD.

e. Even if we can convince the Muslim with these arguments, however, we haven't solved the problem for him! As far as he is concerned, since the New Testament speaks of Jesus as God, or as the Son of God, *it must by definition be corrupted* – regardless of what the Qur'an or Muslim apologists say.

Arguments of this kind, therefore, have limited value unless we can persuade our Muslim friend to read one of the gospels (preferably Luke) with a slightly more open mind. And we will then need to be able to tackle the fundamental issues, ie, the divinity of Christ, the Trinity and the Crucifixion.

9

MUSLIMS AND CONVERSION

This subject should logically be considered after Study 10 – Explaining the Gospel. It is placed here, however, in order to emphasize the need for us to *count the cost* of what we are doing: do we have any idea of what conversion may mean for a Muslim? Do we realize the possible cost for any Muslim who wants to become a disciple of Jesus? Do we realize the possible cost for ourselves?

It is a sad fact that in spite of its tolerant attitudes in many areas, Islam does not find it easy to accept the idea of a Muslim becoming a Christian. Conversion to Christianity (or to any other religion) is generally regarded as apostasy, as a betrayal of one's family and society.

Muslims who express an interest in the Christian faith are often subject to strong pressures; and those who finally take the step of being baptized frequently experience opposition and hostility in the home, at work and in society. Many converts in the past have had to leave their homes for safety, and some have been killed.

I Dared to Call Him Father is a moving account of the conversion of Biliquis Sheikh, a high-born Muslim Pakistani woman. The book ends with her being forced to leave Pakistan:

> "My thoughts were . . . on the realisation that I was leaving my homeland. I felt sad, certainly, but at the same time *complete*. I couldn't understand it. . . .
>
> 'What now, Lord? Again I have such a feeling of *completion!* You have brought me out of my homeland, like Abram. Not knowing what comes next, yet complete. Satisfied, because I am with you.'
>
> Even embarrassment over my fears and nervousness didn't bother me now. All I knew was that I had obeyed the Lord in every way. And I had to admit that I would never really know what might

have happened if I had not followed His command and moved as I did.

Tiny lights whisked by the window and suddenly the rumbling of wheels beneath us ceased. We were airborne! In the light of early dawn, I could see the shoreline of Pakistan on the Indian Ocean receding below us.

I held out my hand to Him. He was my only security. My only joy was staying in His Presence. As long as I could stay there I knew that I would be living in the glory.

'Thank you, God,' I breathed. 'Thank You for letting me travel with You.' "

(*I Dared to Call Him Father,* by Bilquis Sheikh, Kingsway, 1979, pp 168-169)

We therefore need to consider these two questions:

WHAT ARE THE REASONS FOR THESE DIFFICULTIES ASSOCIATED WITH CONVERSION? and
HOW CAN WE HELP A MUSLIM WHO WANTS TO BECOME A DISCIPLE OF JESUS?

WHAT ARE THE REASONS FOR THESE DIFFICULTIES ASSOCIATED WITH CONVERSION?

1. Is it simply that this is the reaction of uneducated and backward communities?

- If this is the reason, we can only hope that intolerance will gradually decrease with the spread of education and knowledge. But the fact that the reaction is fairly similar at all levels of Muslim society suggests that this is not the real or only reason.

2. Is it that Islam cannot tolerate any conversion? Is it because there is a law, written or unwritten, to the effect that any convert can or should be killed?

- If this is the reason, all we can do is to think very soberly about the teaching of Jesus on the cost and the rewards of discipleship, and ask ourselves: would *we* be prepared to pay the price that most Muslim converts have to pay, in terms of loneliness, misunderstanding, persecution and even death?
- Would *we* ourselves be prepared to pay this price *with* any convert?

(See FOR FURTHER STUDY: **The Law of Apostasy,** pp 65ff.)

3. Is it that we are making a mistake in expecting individual Muslims to become Christians?

- If this is the reason, we should be thinking in terms of the conversion of families, and even whole communities, rather than individuals. It may be also that we should begin to think in terms of a mission to Islam as a whole, to the whole "House of Islam", in the same way that we think of our mission to the Jewish People.

4. Is it that we are making a mistake in hoping for *any* conversions, whether of individuals or of families?

- If this is the case, we shouldn't want any Muslim to "become a Christian", but rather help him to become a better Muslim. Or it may be that we need to revise our understanding of "conversion", and distinguish carefully between conversion in the sense of "repentance before God and trust in our Lord Jesus" (Acts 20.21) and conversion in the sense of a total change of the Muslim's position in his society.

5. Is it that the convert himself rejects everything in his culture and religion?

- If this is the reason, or at least part of the reason, we ought to try to help the convert to be less negative, and to see how it may be possible for him to be a genuine and faithful disciple of Jesus within his own community and culture.

6. Is it that Christians by their influence tend to extract the Muslim from his culture and society?

- If this is the reason, we need to recognize that we ourselves are very much part of our own culture. We also need to give the convert as much freedom as possible to find out for himself, under the guidance of the Holy Spirit, what loyalty to Christ will mean for him in his own culture.

HOW CAN WE HELP A MUSLIM WHO WANTS TO BECOME A DISCIPLE OF JESUS?

We have deliberately avoided the expression "become a Christian", because in many situations it has certain definite overtones: it implies that the convert has to cease to be a Muslim in order to become a Christian, and it assumes that he must be totally identified with the Christian community in his society, perhaps even to the extent of changing his religion on his identity card.

We have used the term "become a disciple of Jesus" in order to avoid prejudging the issue, and to leave open the question of how a

Muslim's allegiance to Jesus Christ will affect his position in his community.

The following are some of the issues which he will need to face at some stage. Because of all that is involved, we will probably need to face these issues *with him*. In working through these questions we are trying on the one hand to be faithful to the teaching of Jesus, and on the other to avoid placing unnecessary stumbling blocks in anyone's way.

Relating to the Body of Christ

WELCOMING THE NEW BELIEVER (*Read* Acts 9.10-19)

Q. - How easy was it for Ananias to go to Saul and say "Saul, my brother . . ."? What were the fears and prejudices in Ananias' mind which had to be dealt with?
- What can we do to help the new Muslim believer to feel that he is fully accepted as a brother?

OVERCOMING SUSPICIONS (*Read* Acts 9.26-28)

Q. - Why were the Christians in Jerusalem so suspicious about Saul after his conversion?
- Does this help us to understand *our* suspicions and fears about converted Muslims?
- What would it mean for us to repent of *our* prejudices and *our* lack of love towards converts?
- What was the special role which Barnabas played in this situation?
- What can we do to help converts to feel that they are totally accepted in the community of believers?
- What can we learn from the experience of Muslim converts in the past and their relationships with existing churches?
- Are there situations in which it is so difficult for Muslim converts to join an existing church that they should think of starting a church on their own?

Relationships with his Family

CHRIST AND FAMILY LOYALTIES
(*Read* Luke 14.25-33, Matthew 10.16-23, 34-39, and Mark 10.23-31)

Q. - Will the family be tolerant, critical or hostile?
- Will he be able to remain within the family?

- Is the opposition likely to be such that he will have to leave his family for his own safety or peace of mind?

THE SOLIDARITY OF THE FAMILY

(*Read* Luke 19.9, John 4.39-42, Acts 2.39, 9.32-35, 16.31-34)

Q. - Should we work towards the conversion of the whole family (and even the whole community) and not only of an individual in the family? If so, how?

- If we were to take the principle of the solidarity of the family seriously, how would it affect our approach?

  Would it mean, for example

  - deliberately deciding to meet with the whole family and not just with one individual from the family?
  - addressing ourselves primarily to the head of the family rather than to the children or the wife?
  - delaying baptism of an individual until the whole family is convinced and wants to be baptized?

The Five Pillars

Read the following three incidents in the life of Paul and ask if they shed any light on the question of whether a Muslim can continue to practise any of the Five Pillars, or whether he must inevitably give them all up:

ACTS 16.1-3

Timothy's mother was a Jewess, which made him technically a Jew; but his father was a Gentile, and Timothy had not been circumcised as a child. The Jerusalem decrees had said that it was not necessary for Gentile believers to be circumcised (Acts 15.1-35).

Paul probably expected *Jewish* believers to continue to circumcise their children; but he taught that *Gentile* believers should not ask for circumcision, because this would imply that they were obliged to keep the law of Moses (Galatians 5.2-6).

Paul probably circumcised Timothy *either* because he believed that as a Jew he should have been circumcised, *or* in order to make sure that no Jewish critics could say that Paul had encouraged Jewish believers to abandon the law of Moses.

ACTS 18.18

This was presumably a Nazirite vow (see Numbers 6.18), although Luke does not explain the reason in Paul's mind. This ceremony could have marked the end of a vow Paul had previously taken (perhaps in connection with his mission), or the taking of a new vow (possibly connected with his mission to Jerusalem).

ACTS 21.17-26

The Jewish believers in Jerusalem were still staunch upholders of the Law and were worried at rumours that Paul was encouraging Jewish converts to ignore the Law of Moses. They therefore wanted Paul to prove to the Jews that he was still a devout, practising Jew.

The four men concerned had probably taken a temporary Nazirite vow, like Paul's earlier vow (see 18.18). Paul was not asked to take the vow himself; he simply agreed to pay the expenses of the sacrifice and go through the ritual purification with them.

Q. - What was Paul's motive in each case for carrying out these Jewish rites?

a. Was this something Paul did out of *personal conviction,* because he still considered himself a practising Jew and believed in the value of these rites (even if he didn't expect other Jewish and Gentile believers to practise them)?

b. Was this something Paul did simply as *a concession to the feelings of Jews,* in order to avoid giving them reasons for criticising him?

c. Was this something Paul did *deliberately in order to "live like the Jews",* even though he didn't believe he was any longer subject to the law of Moses? Was his motive evangelistic, "in order to win the Jews"?

- Is there any parallel between the traditions of Judaism and the traditions of Islam? If so, can the example of Paul help us to answer similar questions about Muslim practices? If Paul did not give up everything in his Jewish past, does the Muslim believer have to give up everything in his traditions?

  He will have difficulty in declaring "Muhammad is the apostle of God", and he may have no desire to make the Pilgrimage. But does he have to give up the prescribed prayers, fasting and alms-giving if he feels they are an important part of his worship of God?

Culture

JUDGING OUR CULTURE (*Read* Luke 10.38-42)

According to the thinking of her society, Martha was doing *the correct thing* by preparing a big meal to welcome her distinguished guest. It would have been shocking for her to provide Jesus with an ordinary, simple meal, and she would have lost face with her neighbours. This incident can therefore be seen as an example of Jesus challenging accepted ideas in his own culture.

Q. – Are there things in our culture (whether Indian, Egyptian, American or European, etc) which we feel are challenged by the Gospel?

– The Muslim tends to see everything in life as part of his religion; he cannot separate religion from culture nor the religious from the secular. How can we help the Muslim believer to see ways in which his culture may be judged by the Gospel?

MISDIRECTED EVANGELISTIC ZEAL (*Read* Matthew 23.15)

Q. – Why did Jesus condemn the evangelistic zeal of the Pharisees so strongly?

– Are there ways in which we come under the same condemnation today – eg, by making converts "in our image"?

STAYING WHERE WE BELONG (*Read* Mark 5.1-20)

Q. – Why did Jesus encourage this man to stay among his own people?

– How can we avoid encouraging every convert to become "one of us", to join our group and to come out of his own community?

DISTINGUISHING BETWEEN GOSPEL AND CULTURE
(*Read* Acts 15.28-29)

Q. – What was the central issue at stake at the Council of Jerusalem?

– Why did the Council lay down these basic rulings about converts from non-Jewish backgrounds?

– If the apostles insisted that Gentiles did not have to adopt Jewish religion and culture when they became Christians, should we not insist that the Muslim does not have to adopt our culture when he becomes a disciple of Jesus?

QUESTIONS RELATING TO MARRIAGE
(*Read* 1 Corinthians 7.1-40)

Paul is here dealing with questions about marriage raised by new converts living in a non-Christian society.

Q. – When a Muslim becomes a disciple of Jesus, how will it affect his thinking about marriage and the family (whether he is married or single)?

- Can we apply any of the principles given here to the situation a Muslim convert is likely to face?

(For further study of issues related to culture, see **The Gospel and Culture,** pp 42ff.)

Confession

THE IMPORTANCE OF CONFESSION

(*Read* Matthew 10.32-33; Romans 10.9-10)

Q. - What is the importance of confession for the new believer?
- Does the confession always have to be public? Must the convert always confess his faith openly to his family and friends from the very beginning?

IS A "SECRET DISCIPLE" A CONTRADICTION IN TERMS?

(*Read* John 3.1-10, 7.50-52, 19.38-42, 12.42-43)

Q. - Does the gospel account imply any criticism of Nicodemus, Joseph and other Jews who believed, for being secret disciples?
- Did they in any way deny Jesus by hiding their commitment to him?
- Did their actions amount to a public confession of Jesus?
- Is there any reason why a Muslim convert should not in certain circumstances remain a secret disciple until the time is ripe to declare his faith openly?

LEGITIMATE COMPROMISES? (*Read* 2 Kings 5.15-19)

When Naaman the Syrian was healed, he recognized the uniqueness of Yahweh, the God of Israel. Since he associated Yahweh with the land of Palestine, he asked Elisha if he could take home some soil from the country, so that he could offer sacrifices to Yahweh in his own country. He also asked Elisha about the situation he would face in his work: as commander of the army he would have to attend sacrifices with the king in the temple of the god Rimmon. Although he now recognized the unique claims of Yahweh, would it be unforgiveable compromise for him to fulfil his official obligations and take part in such worship, even though he no longer recognized the god Rimmon?

Q. - What was Elisha's response to these two questions?
- Was Naaman's dilemma similar to the dilemma of the Muslim believer?
- Are there ever circumstances in which the Muslim believer should adopt a similar attitude?

HONESTY AND WISDOM (*Read* Matthew 26.62-64, 27.11-14)

There were at least two occasions when Jesus was very careful in the way he answered direct questions:

When he was on trial before the Sanhedrin, he was silent at first when accusations were brought against him. When he was forced to say whether or not he was the Messiah, the son of God, he gave a careful answer: "The words are yours. But I tell you this . . ." (NEB). If he had answered with a straightforward "Yes", he would have given the impression that he was the kind of political leader which many Jews expected the Messiah to be. He gave the same kind of answer during the trial before Pilate, when he was asked the direct question "Are you the king of the Jews?"

In both these situations Jesus refused to answer some of their accusations. When he did answer, he gave answers which were not a straightforward "Yes" or "No", because he wanted to avoid creating misunderstandings. We believe that Jesus was indeed the Messiah, the son of God, the king of the Jews - but not in the sense that his accusers understood these titles.

Q. - If a Muslim asks a Muslim who believes in Jesus, "Have you become a Christian?" what idea does he have in his mind about the word "Christian" and "becoming a Christian"?

- Should the believer answer with a straightforward "Yes" in spite of the possible misunderstandings? Would it be dishonest if the believer were to give an indirect answer and say, for example, "I am a disciple of Jesus"?
- If a Muslim asks us "Do you believe in the Qur'an"? or "Do you believe Muhammad was a prophet?" how should we answer? We could hardly answer with a simple "Yes"; but a straight "No" would probably close the conversation. How can we be honest but sensitive at the same time?

Baptism

THE SIGNIFICANCE OF BAPTISM

(*Read* Matthew 28.18-20; Mark 16.15-16)

Note that these verses in Mark are from an old ending of the Gospel which is not found in the earliest manuscripts. Even if it is genuine, it should be noted that it does not say that the person who believes but is not baptized will be condemned.

The Jews were familiar with the practice of ceremonial washing for purification. They also baptized proselytes, ie, non-Jews who wanted to accept the faith of Judaism. At the time of Jesus, therefore, the practice of baptism was known, and it was already connected in people's minds with the idea of cleansing from sin. What Jesus did was to take a practice which was already known, and make it a once and for all act of initiation, performed in his name.

The Gentiles were not familiar with the practice of baptism, and it would have been entirely new to them. They would not bring to baptism any negative ideas or misunderstandings from their own background.

To the Muslim, baptism means nothing more nor less than apostasy from Islam. It means that the Muslim has cut himself off from his family and his society; he is renouncing his religion and his community, accepting a new religion and joining a different community.

Q. - Are we to say that every Muslim convert *must* be baptized? Or are there circumstances in which a Muslim convert might delay his baptism - perhaps indefinitely - because *he* does not see baptism in the same light as his Muslim family?

We want Jesus and the message of the cross, and not any secondary issues, to be the only stumbling block. Are there situations in which baptism creates an unnecessary stumbling block for the rest of the Muslim community, because it is seen not only as a sign of public confession of Jesus but as a final repudiation of the Muslim community?

- If Jesus was simply adapting a ceremony already familiar to Jews, could we not on the same principle consider adapting a similar ceremony already known to the Muslim?

The Muslim practises a ceremonial washing before he says his *salāt* five times a day. Is it conceivable that a ceremony similar to the ritual washing could be evolved in which, for example, the Muslim disciple of Jesus has water poured out for him as it would be in the preparation for the ritual prayer? The significant thing in this case, however, would be that the one who pours water for him would do it "in the name of Jesus" and in the presence of the community of believers.

Suffering as a Disciple of Jesus

THE DISCIPLE AND HIS MASTER (*Read* Matthew 10.24-25)

Q. – What kind of treatment does Jesus warn his disciples to expect?

REJOICING IN SUFFERING (*Read* Acts 5.40-42)

Q. – Why were the apostles being persecuted?

– How did they accept this persecution and suffering?

SUFFERING AND GLORY (*Read* 1 Peter 4.12-16)

Q. – How had Peter learned to associate suffering with glory?

– Peter distinguishes carefully between suffering as a Christian and suffering for other reasons. Is it possible to distinguish between the suffering of a convert which is simply because of his allegiance to Jesus Christ, and the suffering which is caused by other secondary things (eg, the convert's attitude to his family and his culture)? Can the Muslim believer understand the difference, even if his community does not?

THE SHAME OF REJECTION (*Read* Hebrews 13.10-14)

Q. – How can the example of Jesus help us when we find ourselves rejected by our own community and covered with shame in their eyes?

FOR FURTHER STUDY

The Law of Apostasy in Islam

1. The following are the main verses in the Qur'an which speak about those who leave the religion of Islam:

2.217; 3.90; 4.89; 5.54; 16.106-107.

2. In their original context in the Qur'an these verses were not concerned with Muslims becoming Christians. Many of them deal with those who are described as "the Hypocrites", ie, people who made a profession of faith in Islam but were not sincere, and then went back to their former beliefs.

A modern commentator, Yusuf Ali, relates the verse 4.89 to the circumstances after the Battle of Uhud:

"When the desertion of the Hypocrites at Uhud nearly caused a disaster to the Muslim cause, there was great feeling among the Muslims of Medina against them. One party wanted to put them to the sword; another to leave them alone. The actual policy pursued avoided both extremes, and was determined by these verses. It was clear that they were a danger to the Muslim community if they were admitted into its counsels, and in any case they were a source of demoralisation. But while every caution was used, no extreme measures were taken against them. On the contrary, they were given a chance of making good. If they made sacrifice for the cause ("flee from what is forbidden"), their conduct purged their previous cowardice, and their sincerity entitled them to be taken back. But if they deserted the Muslim community again, they were treated as enemies, with the additional penalty of desertion which is enforced by all nations actually at war."

3. **Muslim Tradition** *(hadith),* which often has authority for Muslims similar to the authority of Church Tradition for Catholic or Orthodox Christians, tends to be very strict on the question of apostasy, and makes little distinction between different categories of apostates.

This, for example, is one tradition related by Al Bukhari (9th century):

"It is related from Ikrimah that he said, 'Hypocrites were brought to Ali and he burnt them.' The news of that reached Ibn Abbas, and he said, 'If it had been I, I would not have burnt them, because of the prohibition of the Apostle of God: Do not punish with the punishment of God; but I would certainly have killed them according to the word of the Apostle: Whoever changes his religion, kill him.' "

(Samuel Zwemer, *The Law of Apostasy in Islam,* Marshall Brothers, 1924, p 38)

4. **Muslim commentators** give different interpretations of the Qur'anic verses.

For example, Al Baidhawi, the famous commentator of the 13th century, commenting on 4.89:

"Whoever turns back from his belief (*irtada*), openly or secretly, take him and kill him wheresoever ye find him, like any other infidel. Separate yourself from him altogether. Do not accept intercession in his regard."

(quoted in Samuel Zwemer, *The Law of Apostasy in Islam,* p 33f)

Maulvi Muhammad Ali belonged to the Ahmadiyya Movement, which has now been declared a non-Muslim community by the government of Pakistan. His comment on 2.217 probably represents the attitude of many more liberal (but orthodox) Muslims:

"The persons spoken of in this passage are the apostates, or those who 'turn from their religion'. A wrong impression exists among non-Muslims, and among some Muslims as well, that the Holy Qur'an requires those who apostatize from Islam to be put to death, but this is not true. . . . As the plain words of the Qur'an show, what is stated here is that the opponents of Islam exerted themselves to their utmost to turn back the Muslims from their faith by their cruel persecutions, and therefore if a Muslim actually went back to unbelief he would be a loser in this life as well as in the next, because the desertion of Islam would not only deprive him of the spiritual advantages which he could obtain by remaining a Muslim, but also of the physical advantages which must accrue to the Muslims through the triumph of Islam. And neither here nor anywhere else in the Holy Qur'an is there even a hint at the infliction of capital or any other punishment on the apostate."

(*The Holy Qur'an,* Arabic text with English translation and Commentary, Ahmadiyya Anjuman-i-Ishaat-i-Islam, Lahore 1920, pp 98-99)

5. If you know a Muslim well enough to ask him about the Muslim attitude to apostasy, he may well say that there is no such thing as a law concerning it, whether written or unwritten. This may reflect either politeness on his part, or ignorance, or increasing tolerance on the part of educated Muslims. The real test, however, is what actually happens in any Muslim society when a Muslim confesses his allegiance to Jesus Christ.

10

EXPLAINING THE GOSPEL

Assuming that we are relating to Muslims in a positive and loving way (Study 1); that we have begun to listen, to understand and to know more about Islam (Studies 2-8); that we have counted the cost of what we are engaged in (Study 9); and that our Muslim friends want to know about *our* faith, how can we begin to explain the Gospel?

SOME BASIC GUIDELINES

1. There is no single technique for explaining the Gospel to a Muslim. We must resist the temptation to think that one simple method is bound to produce results and save us from much heartache and agony.

(*Read* 2 Corinthians 4.1-2)

2. Don't underestimate the power of personal testimony. If you believe that you know God in a personal way, don't be afraid to say so, and to say why you believe this kind of personal relationship is possible. If you believe your sins have been forgiven, explain the basis of your confidence in God's forgiveness.

(*Read* 1 Thessalonians 2.8)

3. Be content to explain one small aspect of the Gospel at a time. Don't feel you have failed if you have not been able to explain "the whole Gospel" at one time.

(*Read* Matthew 13.3)

4. You can sometimes convey more of the Gospel in an indirect way than in a direct way. For example, talking about the meaning of human love can lead to discussion about the love of God. A book like Walter Trobisch's *I Married You* may speak to the heart much more than a book of apologetics addressed directly to the intellect.

5. Make it a priority to encourage your friend at the appropriate time to read one of the gospels. If he says that the Bible has been corrupted, say that you are willing to discuss the question; but ask him if he has ever *read* the Bible himself.

Luke is perhaps the best gospel to start with.

Matthew is also valuable, but some Muslims may find it difficult because it is so Jewish.

Mark introduces a stumbling block in the very first sentence by speaking of Jesus as "the son of God".

John may be more helpful at a later stage.

USING THE SCRIPTURES

The remainder of this study is based on the series of Scripture Passages entitled "*The Message of the Tawrat, the Zabur and the Injil – Selected Passages from the Holy Bible*" (published in English, French and Arabic by the Bible Society in Lebanon, and obtainable from the British and Foreign Bible Society, 146 Queen Victoria Street, London EC4V 4BX).

The following notes suggest how the passages can be explained to a Muslim. When you have completed these studies, you may want to give the Selections to a Muslim friend and, if possible, study them with him. You may want to give them all together, or one or two at a time.

1. God is One and has Created Man to Serve and Love Him

In the first few studies of this series we are trying to build bridges with the Muslim by studying truths which *he also* believes, even if he expresses them in a slightly different way. We are also trying to lay foundations for the later studies by giving a clear idea of God as a personal God who is loving and holy.

We therefore begin with passages which speak about the oneness of God and the rejection of idolatry. We want to assure the Muslim that we believe in the oneness of God as strongly as he does. The Ten Commandments (Exodus 20.3-5) begin with a condemnation of idolatry and what the Muslim calls *shirk* (ie, the sin of associating anything created with God the Creator).

Jesus' summary of the OT law emphasizes the oneness of God and our obligation to love him (Mark 12.29-30).

Other parts of the Bible warn against idolatry in different ways:

Paul condemns idolatry along with other serious sins (Galatians 5.19-21);

John includes idolatry among the sins which deserve judgment in hell (Revelation 21.8).

Psalm 33.1, 4-9 and Psalm 105.1-6 call us to worship God as the one who has revealed himself through his mighty acts in creation and in history.

Psalm 95.1-7 and 139.1-6, 13-14 are prayers of worship, which express the believer's joy and thankfulness, his reverence for God and his confidence in him as a personal God.

2. God gives Man His Laws

It is often said that the Muslim has a superficial understanding of sin. The importance of this study is therefore that it outlines clearly the moral law that God has laid down for us all. We cannot hope to understand the meaning of sin, or feel any guilt or shame before God, unless we know the standards he has set for us, and begin to realize how far short we have fallen.

The Muslim is not likely to find any problem in the Ten Commandments (Exodus 20.1-17). The Qur'an contains similar moral teaching in different places, but it is not summed up so clearly or concisely as in the Ten Commandments.

The teaching of Jesus builds on the Ten Commandments in several ways:

- it summarizes the demands of the law in terms of loving God and loving our neighbour (Matthew 22.34-40).
- it shows that the law applies not only to outward actions but also to our inward thoughts and motives (Matthew 5.21-24).
- it shows that God's standards are very much higher than the moral standards of most societies (Matthew 5.43-45).

Psalm 119.1-16 expresses the desire of the believer to surrender himself completely to God and to obey his revealed law.

3. God warns Man of the Consequences of Failure to keep His Laws

The Qur'an has its own version of the story of Adam and Eve in the Garden of Eden (see Surah 2.30-39; 7.19-27; 20.115-122). The Muslim may therefore be interested to read the biblical version of this story (Genesis 2.8-9, 15-17; 3.1-13; 3.22-24). He may appreciate that Adam and Eve's awareness of their nakedness indicates the sense of shame which they felt after their sin.

Ezekiel 18.1-4, 30-32 emphasizes the responsibility of the individual before God. Though we are affected by the results of the sins of our parents, we are not held responsible or punished for their sins. Each person is responsible before God for what he has done.

Romans 3.9-20, 23 emphasizes the seriousness of sin its universality and its power. Sin is very much more than individual mistakes; it is a complete turning away from God, which affects every part of our lives and puts us "under God's judgment", and "far away from God's saving presence". This applies to us *all,* whatever our race or religion. The law is unable to provide a final answer, since it cannot restore the broken relationship; all it can do is to make us more aware of our helpless condition.

Psalm 51.1-9 shows the meaning of true repentance in one who realizes that he has broken the commandments of God and has no right to expect God's forgiveness.

4. God is Merciful and Loving and wants to Forgive

Psalm 103.8-14 gives content to the belief that God is merciful, and in this context we are introduced to the idea of God being like a Father. If this sounds very foreign to the Muslim (because it speaks of God in such human terms), it may be helpful to point out that there is a verse in the Qur'an in which God says about Adam: "I have made him and have breathed into him of My spirit" (15.29). There is also a well known tradition (*hadīth*) which says: "God created Adam upon his own form" (where the Arabic is the same as the traditional Arabic translation of Genesis 1.28).

Leviticus 9.7 and 16.5-10, 21-22 introduces the subject of sacrifice in the OT, in order to show that in God's dealings with men, forgiveness is not just a matter of words; he does not forgive simply by pronouncing a divine pardon. Many of the animal sacrifices in the OT period were offered "to take away the sins of the people". If these assumptions can be understood at this stage, it will help us later when we come to consider the difficult subject of the death of Jesus.

The parable of the Pharisee and the Publican (Luke 18.9-14) can be adapted in such a way that it expresses what devout Muslims may feel: "I say the *salāt* five times a day; I fast during Ramadān; I give *zakāt;* I've been on Pilgrimage. . . ."

Jeremiah 5.7, 9 and Hosea 11.8-9 open up the question of *how* God forgives, and point to the need for atonement. In Jeremiah God says, in effect, "How can I avoid punishing my people?" while in Hosea he says "How can I bring myself to punish them in the way that they really deserve?" We therefore begin to feel something of the tension in the heart of God between his love and his holiness. This tension is only resolved in the death and resurrection of Jesus. We shall see later that if the Muslim can understand *the reason why* God could allow Jesus to suffer and die on the cross, he is more likely to be willing to accept *the fact that* he did die on the cross.

Psalm 32.1-7 expresses the joy of the believer who knows that his sins are forgiven. Some Muslims are confident that if they confess their sins and live a good life they will be forgiven. The vast majority, however, would have to admit that they cannot be sure that their sins have been forgiven. They will not know until the Day of Judgment, when their good deeds will be weighed in the balance against their bad deeds.

5. God Revealed to His Prophets that He Would Come Among Men

In this study we are trying to prepare for the idea of the Incarnation by showing that in the OT God says that he wants to live among men. Instead of emphasizing Messianic prophecies which speak of *a man* whom God is going to raise up, we concentrate on passages which speak about *God himself* coming among men.

Isaiah 55.10-11 speaks of God coming among men in his word: his word is, so to speak, an extension of himself, and it is through his word that he acts in the world. In traditional Muslim theology there has been a great deal of discussion about the status of the word of God, and some Christians have found this a way of introducing the idea of Jesus as the eternal Word of God. (See Surah 3.45 and 4.171.)

Leviticus 26.1-2, 11-12; Exodus 29.44-45 and Ezekiel 37.26-27 show that the Tabernacle and the Temple were intended to be a sign of God living among his people.

Similarly Malachi 3.1 and Isaiah 40.3-5 speak of God himself coming to reveal himself and proclaim his covenant.

Micah 5.2 is the only "Messianic" prophecy included here.

Psalm 96.10-13 expresses the joy and confidence of the believer who knows that God is coming to establish his justice and his kingly rule on earth.

Isaiah 64.1-9 is a prayer that God will come down to reveal himself and show mercy to sinful and rebellious men in a way that is even clearer than the great exodus from Egypt.

6. God sent Jesus the Messiah as His Word through a Miraculous Birth and gave Him Miraculous Powers

The Muslim should find no difficulty in the title of this study. Jesus is mentioned in 93 verses of the Qur'an with different names and titles: eg, 'Isa (ie, Jesus – 25 times); al-Masih – (ie, the Christ, the Messiah – 11 times); son of Mary (23 times). The Qur'an has its own accounts of the birth and ministry of Jesus, and the Muslim who knows them will no doubt notice how they differ from the NT accounts (Matthew 1.18-25 and Luke 2.1-20):

the annunciation to Mary, 3.45-50; 19.16-21.
the birth of Jesus, 19.22-37; 21.91.
the miracles of Jesus, 2.87; 5.110-117.
the disciples of Jesus, 3.52-54; 5.111.

Three miracles of Jesus have been selected here, each for a different reason:

- The reaction of the disciples after the stilling of the storm shows how their faith in Jesus grew gradually: "who is this man . . .?" (Luke 8.22-25).
- There are certain similarities between the feeding of the 5,000 (Luke 9.10-17) and a passage in the Qur'an (5.111-115), where the disciples of Jesus ask him: "Is thy Lord able to send down for us a table spread with food from heaven?"
- Jesus' ability to cast out evil spirits demonstrates his power over all the forces of evil (Luke 4.31-37). Our proclamation of Jesus must show what he is able to *do,* and what he is able to do for us *now.* Many Muslims have come to faith in Christ largely through experiencing his power in some dramatic way in their lives.

The value of Luke 7.18-23 is that the message which Jesus sent to John points to *what he was doing* (healing, raising the dead, preaching, etc) as a sign of *who he was.* Although the Qur'an speaks of Jesus as "the Messiah", it gives no indication of the meaning of the title. We therefore seek to show what the NT means by the title: Jesus was chosen and anointed by God for a special ministry among men. John the Baptist is known in the Qur'an as Yayha (eg, 3.37-41).

The Song of Mary (Luke 1.46-55) links the birth of Jesus with the covenant promises made to Abraham and the Children of Israel. The Muslim has great respect for the Virgin Mary, because of the Qur'anic verse: "O Mary! Lo! Allah hath chosen thee and made thee pure, and hath preferred thee above (all) the women of creation" (3.42).

In this study and the next we have deliberately not included passages which speak of Jesus as "the Son of God", because the title is open to such misunderstanding, and because our proclamation of Jesus as the one who was both man and God need not depend on this one single title. We ought to be able to find, from within the NT, different ways of helping the Muslim to see that Jesus was more than a prophet. (See **For further study: Jesus "the Son of God"** pp 77ff.)

7. God gave Jesus the Messiah the Message of the Injīl (the Gospel)

The Qur'an speaks of the *injīl* as the message which was revealed to Jesus (eg, 5.46-47), but it gives no indication of what it was about. This study is therefore intended to give some idea of the content of the Gospel which Jesus proclaimed.

Mark 1.14-15 and Luke 4.16-19 are brief summaries of the message in the words of Jesus himself.

The importance of Luke 5.17-26 is that it concentrates our attention on what Jesus actually did: he healed the sick man and at the same time claimed to be able to forgive sins. The thoughtful Muslim will no doubt react to this claim in the same way as the Pharisees did; but at least he should see that our understanding of Jesus is based on what he said and did and not on later theology developed by Paul and others.

The parable of the Prodigal Son (Luke 15.11-32) can be specially valuable for the Muslim, because of its emphasis on God as a loving Father who welcomes his son back home, and suffers as he forgives all the wrongs that have been done to him. It is also helpful because it shows the difference between worshipping God as a slave or servant (as the Muslim seeks to do) and worshipping him as a son. The parable insists that God is not content that we should worship him as slaves and wants us to have the status of sons. The parable has no ending; we are not told whether the older brother accepted his father's invitation. God therefore leaves each of us free to accept or reject his invitation to live as sons who recognize him as Father.

The Lord's Prayer (Matthew 6.9-13) is included here because it shows that Jesus encouraged his disciples to pray to God as sons addressing a loving Father. We can point out that the prayer is recited by some Christians rather as the Fātihah is recited by Muslims.

8. God Demonstrated His Love for Sinful Men through the Death of Jesus the Messiah

Because the crucifixion is such a difficult subject to discuss with the Muslim, the title attempts to put it in the context of the love of God.

We are trying to concentrate not just on *the* fact of the crucifixion, but on the *reasons* for it, by showing how it can be seen as a demonstration of the love of God.

It is important to understand exactly what it is that the Muslim denies in the story of the crucifixion:

he does *not deny* that the Jews wanted to kill Jesus;
he does *not deny* that Jesus was willing to be killed;
he *denies only* that God allowed Jesus to be crucified.

John 5.15-18 explains the reason for the hostility of the Jews towards Jesus, which is not explained in the Qur'an: it was partly because they believed Jesus was breaking the law, but primarily because, by speaking of God as "my Father", he "made himself equal with God".

Luke 22.41-44 shows that Jesus was willing to be captured and killed.

In Matthew 26.51-54 we see that Jesus believed that God *could* rescue him from death if he wanted to. Jesus, however, had understood from the OT scriptures that it was necessary for him to die. From his time in the wilderness, Jesus had come to see the idea of a miraculous deliverance from death as a Satanic temptation (Matthew 4.5-7). Even while he hung on the cross he was taunted by onlookers who said they would believe in him if he were rescued in a miraculous way; but he resisted the temptation right to the very end (Matthew 27.39-43).

In Luke 22.66 - 23.2 we see that the Jews finally decided to kill Jesus because they thought his claims about himself amounted to blasphemy. The orthodox Muslim is likely to react in exactly the same way, because he sees such claims as *shirk,* ie, the sin of associating something created with God.

Before we find ourselves trying to convince the Muslim that Jesus was actually crucified, we should encourage him to read this straightforward account of how Jesus is reported to have died (Luke 23.20-26; 32-43; 44-49).

Isaiah 53.4-6 introduces us to the Suffering Servant who bears the sins of men. We have already noticed (p 71) that the sacrificial system in the OT speaks of *animals* being offered in sacrifice and bearing the sins of men. Here we find that a *person* is said to have "borne our sins", and taken "the punishment all of us deserved".

Psalm 22.1-19 is the prayer of one who feels that God has abandoned him. We believe that when Jesus used the words of verse 1 (and presumably the whole psalm) as he hung on the cross, his prayer was answered: but instead of being rescued *before* death, he was rescued *after* death. The basic difference, therefore, between the Christian and Muslim understanding of the crucifixion is that while the Muslim believes that God vindicated Jesus by rescuing him in a miraculous way before he was crucified, the Christian believes that God vindicated him after he was crucified by raising him from death and thus breaking the power of death.
(For further discussion of the crucifixion, see **FOR FURTHER STUDY: The Death of Jesus,** p 81 ff.)

9. God Raised Jesus from Death

Most of this study consists of Luke's account of the discovery of the empty tomb (Luke 23.50-56 and 24.1-12) and the appearances of the risen Jesus to the disciples (Luke 24.13-35; 36-47).

The story of the appearance to the two disciples on the road to Emmaus is specially valuable because it shows how Jesus had to explain to the disciples the necessity of his suffering and death: "was it not necessary for the Messiah to suffer these things and then to enter his glory?" The disciples may well have had the same idea as the Muslim: how could God possibly have allowed his Messiah to suffer and be killed in this way?

Hebrews 2.14-18 explains another aspect of the divine logic which demanded that Jesus should suffer and die: "he had to become like his brothers in every way . . .". How could Jesus help us when we face temptation, suffering and death itself, if he were protected by God in a special way and miraculously delivered from death? What kind of sympathy could he have with us? We believe that Jesus is able to help us because he faced all the powers of evil; he experienced the worst that men and the Devil could do to him; and by going through death he has broken the hold that it has over men.

Psalm 16.1-11 expresses the believer's confidence that in the life beyond death he will have the joy of being in God's presence. The Muslim may well notice how this differs from the Qur'an's understanding of heaven (or Paradise).

10. God Gave His Spirit to the Disciples who Recognized Jesus as God's Messiah and God's Word

The Qur'an contains references to the Spirit of God: eg, 17.85; 70.4; 78.38 and 97.4. The Spirit is often associated with revelation and inspiration: eg, 16.102; 42.52. The Spirit is also associated with Jesus 2.87, 253; 4.171; 5.110.

Acts 1.2-5; 8-9 shows how the coming of the Spirit was closely related to Jesus and his ascension to the Father in heaven.

Acts 1.10-11 states that God raised Jesus to himself – not, as the Muslim believes, in a miraculous intervention before death, but after his death and resurrection, as a final vindication of all that he had said and done. It also asserts that Jesus is going to come again – a conviction which most Muslims also hold.

Acts 2.1-14 describes how the Holy Spirit first came to the disciples of Jesus.

Acts 2.22-36 is the account of how Peter explained the coming of the Spirit on the Day of Pentecost. Here we have the first Christian attempt to describe in words the relationship between God, Jesus and the Spirit.

Romans 8.1-17 is included here for two main reasons: (a) the Muslim tends to have a much more optimistic view of human nature than the Christian, because he believes that all men are born innocent and only need the revelation of God's law to reveal the right way to live. Here, however, Paul emphasizes man's inability to save himself, and teaches that God's provision for man's fallen human nature includes the incarnation, the atonement and the giving of the Holy Spirit to enable us to obey the law. (b) It is because of the work of God's Spirit in our hearts that we are able to know God as Father. Discussion about Jesus as the Son of God is therefore lifted out of the area of controversy and put in the context of our experience of God. Jesus addressed God as "Abba, Father" and, when we trust in Jesus, the Spirit within us gives us the confidence to address God in the same way.

Psalm 51.10-17. If the Muslim is able to pray this prayer, he is expressing genuine repentance and faith. Even if he is not yet able to articulate his faith in precisely the same way that we can, he may have come to believe that it is only through Jesus that we can enjoy this kind of relationship with God.

FOR FURTHER STUDY

Jesus "the Son of God"

How can we remove misunderstandings about this difficult title? How can we begin to convey what *we* understand by it? Can we find guidelines from both the Bible and the Qur'an?

1. We reject the idea of Jesus being the son of God in any physical sense as strongly as the Muslim does. The idea of Jesus being born of a union between God and the Virgin Mary is utterly abhorrent to us as Christians. If this is what Muhammad understood by the term, it is as blasphemous to us as it is to the Muslim.

See Surah 112.1-4; 19.34-35.

2. Jesus was careful to avoid misunderstandings over names and titles. Although the word "Messiah" came from the OT, the idea had been distorted by the Jews in their speculation about the coming Messianic Age. Since Jesus never described himself as the Messiah, it must have been because he refused to conform to the popular conception of the Messiah as a political and military figure. He preferred to speak of himself as "the son of Man" (a title almost certainly taken from Daniel 7.13ff) and the Suffering Servant (from Isaiah 53, etc). Thus when Peter confessed that Jesus was the *Messiah,* Jesus went on to say "*the son of Man* must suffer . . ." (Mark 8.31).

Similarly when the High Priest asked "are you the *Messiah*?" Jesus answered: "So you say. But I tell you: from this time on you will see the *son of Man . . .* " (Matthew 26.63-64). It was as if Jesus was saying, "I am not the Messiah in the sense that *you* understand the word. And because the term is so open to misunderstandings, I prefer to speak of myself as the 'son of Man'."

When Pilate asked the similar question "are you the king of the Jews?" Jesus answered: "So you say" (Matthew 27.11). In John's version, Jesus went on to define his ministry in terms of declaring the truth.

If Jesus avoided the term Messiah so deliberately, we today have every justification for avoiding the title "son of God" as much as we can in speaking with Muslims. It is *not* dishonest and it is not a dangerous compromise to try to find *other* ways of speaking about Jesus.

3. Our belief in Jesus as the Son of God is based on the words and actions of Jesus himself, and not only on the teaching of Paul and the other apostles.

When Muslims say it was Paul and the early Christians who corrupted the simple *injīl* which Jesus proclaimed, we need to show that Paul's teaching was based on Jesus' teaching; Jesus said and did things which amounted to a claim that he was equal with God:

a. he said he would one day judge all men (Matthew 25.31-46; John 5.22-23).

b. he said he could give men eternal life (John 5.19-21; 11.25-26).

c. he forgave sins (Mark 2.5-7).

d. he called God "Father" or "my Father" and when speaking to his disciples spoke of "your Father". He never spoke of "our Father". He therefore made a clear distinction between his own relationship with God and his disciples' relationship with God (Matthew 12.50; 6.6; John 20.17).

There are at least two important ideas implied in this Father-son relationship: (a) Jesus was claiming to know God in a unique way (Matthew 11.25-27), (b) Jesus claimed to be completely obedient to the will of God (John 8.27-29; 55).

When the Jews heard him speaking of God as his Father, they understood that he was claiming to be equal with God, and it was this claim which was one of the main reasons for the opposition which led to his death.

There are about 150 verses in the Gospels in which Jesus speaks of God as "Father". They are an integral part of the teaching of Jesus, and cannot be cut out without changing the whole message.

4. The first disciples were not pagans who believed in many gods, but orthodox Jews who believed in the oneness of God. As Orthodox Jews they would have been brought up to recite these words from the *shema'* daily: "Hear, O Israel, the Lord our God is one Lord . . ." (Deuteronomy 6.4). They were therefore as convinced monotheists as Muslims are.

At first they followed Jesus simply as a rabbi, a teacher. When they were impressed by his miraculous powers, they still thought of him as an ordinary man: "who is *this man*? Even the wind and the waves obey him!" (Mark 4.41). But when he said and did things that only God can do, they had to find some way of saying that he was in a much closer relationship to God than that of a prophet or any other ordinary human being. Their belief in Jesus developed gradually, and it was a long time before they were able to formulate their convictions about him in precise theological language.

5. The Apostles used many different names to speak about Jesus. In the NT period, a person could express his belief in the deity of

Christ and commit himself to Christ in many different ways, without necessarily using the title "Son of God".

TERMS WHICH WOULD BE UNDERSTOOD BY JEWS:

Lord, Acts 2.36
Christ, Acts 2.36
the Prince of life, Acts 3.15
thy holy servant, Acts 4.27
the Word, John 1.1
the wisdom of God, 1 Corinthians 1.24
the image of the invisible God, Colossians 1.15
the firstborn of all creation, Colossians 1.15
the man from heaven, 1 Corinthians 15.49

TERMS WHICH WOULD BE UNDERSTOOD BY GENTILES:

God's secret (mystery), Colossians 2.2
Lord (Gk *kurios*), Romans 10.9
the one whom God has appointed
  judge of the living and the dead, Acts 10.43
a man he has chosen, Acts 17.31
Saviour (Gk *soter*)

6. It is because Jesus is the Son of God in a unique sense that we can become sons of God.

If the Qur'an encourages us to think of ourselves as slaves or servants of God, the New Testament offers us the possibility of becoming sons of God - sons who know, love and obey God as Father. Jesus spoke of God as "my Father" and shocked his contemporaries by addressing God as *abba* (almost the familiar "Father" or "Daddy"). The wonder of the Gospel is that Jesus also gave his disciples the right to address God as "our Father" (Matthew 6.9). Paul shows the same familiarity in speaking of God as *abba* (Romans 8.15). When we trust in Jesus, he gives us the right to *become* sons of God (John 1.12-13).

The question about Jesus as the Son of God is therefore not simply a theoretical or theological issue; it affects our understanding of who we are and the kind of relationship God wants us to enjoy with him.

7. Starting Points in the Qur'an. The Qur'an provides starting points which can help us in speaking about Jesus. Although it frequently says that God makes no difference between the prophets, there are many ways in which Jesus, son of Mary, is quite unique among the prophets. But what are the reasons for this uniqueness?

- why was he born of a virgin?
- why did he work miracles?
- why was he given titles which no other apostle or prophet was given?

eg, "exalted (above others) in degree . . . supported . . . by the Holy Spirit" (2.253)
"a messenger of Allah, and His word which he conveyed unto Mary, and a spirit from Him" (4.171-172)
"illustrious in the world and the Hereafter, and one of those brought near (unto Allah)" (3.45)

We can ask the Muslim to give his explanation of the uniqueness of Jesus, and offer our explanation from the *injīl*.

Many Christians have found that one of the most fruitful bridges in the Qur'an is the description of Jesus as "a messenger of Allah, and *his Word* which he conveyed to Mary, and *a spirit* from him". A person's words are a part of him - they express his mind and his will. Thus, if we cannot separate a person's words from the person who utters them, we cannot separate Jesus from God. Jesus is the word of God, not (as Muslims generally teach) in the sense that he was created by divine *fiat*, by the word of God, but in the sense that he is the one who expresses the mind and will of God most fully to men. Through Jesus, God has spoken and acted in a unique way.

The Death of Jesus

The crucial passage in the Qur'an about the crucifixion is 4.156-159. The traditional interpretation of this passage is that God raised Jesus up to heaven in a miraculous way before he was actually crucified, and that someone else who looked like him was crucified in his place. There are at least two ways of approaching this difficult text:

1. It can be argued that the Qur'an does not actually deny the crucifixion; all it denies is that it was *the Jews* who carried out the crucifixion.

A verse in another surah refers in similar terms to the victory of the Muslims over the forces of Mecca at the Battle of Badr:

> "Ye (Muslims) slew them not, but Allah slew them. And thou (Muhammad) threwest not when thou didst throw, but Allah threw, that He might test the believers by a fair test from Him" (8.17).

David Brown gives the following explanation of how the reference to the crucifixion in 4.156-157 can be explained in the light of this verse:

"These verses are intended to be a rebuke to the Jews, and particularly to Muhammad's contemporaries in Medina, for various acts of unbelief, and they only refer in passing to the story of the crucifixion. Within this context of an attack on the Jews for their opposition towards Muhammad as well as for other acts of unbelief, the reference to the crucifixion does no more than dispute the claim made by the Jews that they had disposed of the Christian Messiah and repudiated his claims to be an apostle of God by crucifying him.

"In particular, the phrases 'they did not kill him, nor did they crucify him' do not necessarily mean that there was no crucifixion, but that, even if there was, it was God who was responsible for all that happened during the last hours of the Messiah's life and that the Jews had done whatever they did only by permission of God's will. A similar figure of speech occurs in 8.17 (quoted above) in which the Muslim's actions at the Battle of Badr are attributed to God and not to their own volition; they did in fact fight and kill, but only by God's permission and direction.

"These verses, therefore, do not explicitly deny the Christian story of the crucifixion, for they refer primarily to Jewish claims against the Christians. . . ."

(David Brown, *The Cross of the Messiah,* SPCK, 1969, pp 31-32)

This interpretation may be supported by three other passages in the Qur'an which appear to speak about the death of Jesus and suggest by implication that he died like every other human being:

(i) In the account of the birth of Jesus, the infant Jesus speaks to the people from the cradle:
"Peace on me the day I was born, and the day I die, and the day I shall be raised alive!" (19.33)

Similar words are used in the same surah (19.15) about John the Baptist, where they presumably refer to his death and to the general resurrection of all men.

(ii) In another passage God says to Jesus:
"O Jesus! Lo! *I am gathering thee* and causing thee to ascend unto Me, and am cleansing thee of those who disbelieve and am setting those who follow thee above those who disbelieve until the Day of Resurrection." (3.55)

(iii) In the third verse Jesus is speaking to God:
"I spake unto them only that which Thou commandest me (saying): Worship Allah, my Lord and your Lord. I was a

> witness of them while I dwelt among them, and *when Thou tookest* me Thou wast the Watcher over them." (5.117)

The underlined words in the last two passages are forms of the same Arabic word *tawaffa*. The first passage could also be translated "Truly I am he who calls you to death" or "It is I who am causing you to die."

David Brown comments:

> "Both these verses refer to the return of Jesus to God at the end of his life, and the most straightforward interpretation of them is to suppose that they refer to a natural death of Jesus at the end of his earthly life. *Tawaffa* is often used in the Qur'an in the sense of bringing a soul to God at death, both when the subject of the verb is God (eg, 3.193; 10.46), and when the subject is the angels (eg, 16.28, 32). The word *tawaffa,* however, was originally used of a person receiving the full payment of his due or his rights, and when used of God in the Qur'an refers to men being called to pay their account in his presence, either at death, or in sleep when the soul comes to God but is returned to the body for a further term of life on earth. . . .
>
> "Thus the use of the word *tawaffa* in these two passages with reference to the Messiah, is ambiguous and its exact meaning must be determined by consideration of other verses in the Qur'an: it could mean that Jesus died a natural death, but it can also mean that he was taken to heaven without undergoing the experience of physical death" (pp 29-30).

If these three verses, therefore, are interpreted as meaning that Jesus died a natural death on the cross, and if the crucial passage in 4.156-159 is taken to mean only that it was the Romans who crucified Jesus, not the Jews, we may be able to argue from the text of the Qur'an that it does not in fact deny that Jesus died on the cross.

It is significant that the early commentators were not agreed about the interpretation of these verses. It would appear that for several centuries there was considerable debate among Muslims about the crucifixion, and that many different answers were given by orthodox Muslims.

Some Muslims today, who are more liberal in their approach but still consider themselves to be orthodox Muslims, reject all theories about a substitute being crucified in the place of Jesus. For example, Kamel Husein writes in the introduction to his book *City of Wrong.*

"The idea of a substitute for Christ is a very crude way of explaining the Qur'anic text. They had to explain a lot to the masses. No cultured Muslim believes in this nowadays. The text is taken to mean that the Jews thought they killed Christ, but God raised him unto him in a way we can leave unexplained among the several mysteries which we have taken for granted on faith alone" (p 222).

The main difficulty of this first approach is that, however careful and convincing our exegesis of the Qur'an may be, it goes against the traditional teaching which most Muslims today have received about the Crucifixion. If some more open-minded Muslims are willing to accept this interpretation, the vast majority accept as dogma that *Jesus was not crucified.*

2. Another approach to the question of the crucifixion in the Qur'an can be outlined as follows:

a. We should accept the traditional Muslim interpretation that these verses (4.156-159) deny that Jesus was crucified; and accept the possibility that the Qur'an may not be entirely consistent with itself (ie, some verses may suggest a natural death, while others suggest a miraculous deliverance).

b. It should be noted that before the time of Muhammad there were heretical Christian sects which taught that Jesus was not crucified. Muhammad may have heard the idea from sources of this kind.

Geoffrey Parrinder writes:

"There early arose in some Christian circles a reluctance to believe that Jesus, as a divine being and Son of God, could really die. Ignatius, writing about AD 115, said that some believed that Jesus 'suffered in semblance'. The apocryphal Gospel of Peter in the second century said that on the cross Jesus was silent, since he 'felt no pain', and at the end 'the Lord cried out, saying, "My power, my power, you have left me". And when he spoke he was taken up. . . .' The apocryphal Acts of John, about the middle of the second century, said that Jesus appeared to John in a cave during the crucifixion and said, 'John, unto the multitude below in Jerusalem I am being crucified and pierced with lances and reeds, and gall and vinegar is given to me to drink. But unto thee I speak.' And later it is said, 'Nothing, therefore of the things which they will say of me have I suffered . . . I was pierced, yet I was not smitten; hanged, and I was not hanged; that blood flowed from me, and it flowed not'."

(*Jesus in the Qur'an,* p 109)

Some of these ideas were found in the teaching of the Docetics (from the Greek word meaning "to appear"), who taught that the suffering of Jesus was apparent, not real.

c. If this was the background to the denial of the crucifixion in the Qur'an, it might explain the difficult phrase *shubbiha lahum* ("it appeared so to them"). If Muhammad first heard the idea from heretical Christian circles of this kind, he may have accepted it, not because he accepted their docetic teaching but because the idea of Jesus not being crucified fitted his concept of the inviolability of the Apostles of God, and his idea of the uniqueness of Jesus.

   We should try to understand the logic behind the Muslim's denial of the crucifixion. All God's Apostles were regarded as being inviolable - ie, it was unthinkable that God would allow any of them to be killed. This would be true especially for Jesus, because he was in many ways unique among the Apostles and Prophets: he was born of a virgin, worked miracles, and was the "Word" of God and "a Spirit from Him".

   If a government must protect its ambassador in a foreign country and will not stand by idly if he is insulted publicly, God cannot stand by idly if his Apostles are treated shamefully. He must step in to vindicate them, for in vindicating their honour he is vindicating his own honour.

d. Finally, we should try to help the Muslim to see the deeper logic which demands that the Messiah *must* suffer before entering his glory.

   The Muslim believes that forgiveness depends only on God's mercy and man's repentance and belief. There is no need for any sacrifice or atonement. We believe that forgiveness involves suffering. God cannot simply forgive, as it were by decree, since this kind of forgiveness undermines the divine law. How can God forgive the sinner and uphold the law at the same time?

   We can use the experience of the first disciples, and notice how Jesus had to explain the necessity of his sufferings and death to his disciples (Luke 24. 25-27, 44-47).

   If the Muslim can in this way begin to see the *reason* why God could allow Jesus to be crucified, he may be more willing to accept the *fact* that he was crucified.

RESOURCE BOOKS

Translations of the Qur'an

M. Marmaduke Pickthall	*The Meaning of the Glorious Koran,* An Explanatory Translation Mentor Books, published by the New American Library, 1301 Avenue of the Americas, N. York 10019. Perhaps the most readable English translation, made by an English Muslim convert. It has a helpful introduction to each surah and a very useful index. Some are critical of certain aspects of the translation, eg, its use of "Allah" for God.
Arthur J. Arberry	*The Koran Interpreted* Oxford University Press A more literary and poetic translation by the famous English orientalist, which reads like the King James Version. Includes a useful appendix. This is the translation preferred by many orientalists.
A. Yusuf Ali	*The Holy Qur'an,* Text, Translation and Commentary. Translated and published in Pakistan, and now being widely distributed by Muslim missions.
N. J. Dawood	*The Koran* Penguin A very readable translation, but difficult to use because the verse numbers are not given, and the order of the surahs has been rearranged.
J. M. Rodwell	*The Koran, Translated from the Arabic* Everyman's Library, Dent.

Shorter Studies and Booklets written by Christians

Christian Witness Among Muslims
Africa Christian Press, IVP (1971), 96pp.
An excellent handbook, produced originally in West Africa.

Vivienne Stacey — *Practical Lessons for Evangelism Among Muslims*
(published in English and German).
Orientdienst PO Box 4546, 6200 Wiesbaden, West Germany.

C. R. Marsh — *Share Your Faith With A Muslim*
Moody (1973), 95 pp.

John Crossley — *Explaining the Gospel to Muslims*
USCL, Lutterworth (1964), 48 pp.

G. E. Morrison — *The Christian Approach to the Muslim*
Edinburgh House Press (1964), 64pp.

Reaching Muslims Today, A Short Handbook
North Africa Mission, Devonshire Square, Loughborough, England (1977), 64 pp.

Jack Budd — *Studies on Islam, A Simple Outline of the Islamic Faith*
Red Sea Mission Team, 33-35 The Grove, Finchley, London N3 1QU, 60 pp.

John Elder — *The Biblical Approach to the Muslim*
Christian Communications Ltd, PO Box 5364, Hong Kong, 95 pp.

William Miller — *Beliefs and Practices of Christians, A Letter to A Friend*
MIK, 36 Ferozepur Rd, Lahore, Pakistan (1975), 80 pp.

Abd-ul-Masih — *Islam and Christianity, 90 Questions Answered*
Daystar Press, PO Box 4045, Ibadan, Nigeria, 43 pp.

Herbert Spencer — *Islam and the Gospel of God*
ISPCK, Post Box 1585, Kashmere Gate, Delhi - 110006, India (1956).

Emory Van Gerpen — *Notes on Islam*
Challenge Publications, PMB 2010, Jos, Nigeria (1975).

Ray G. Register — *Dialogue and Interfaith Witness with Muslims*
WEC Muslim Ministries, Box A, Fort Washington, PA 19034, USA (1980), 99 pp.

A. H. Whitehouse — *Introduction to Islam*
MECO, 15 Vista Avenue, E Ringwood, Melbourne, Australia, 3135 (1981), 91 pp.
An excellent course of programmed instruction material.

Books on Islam Written by Muslims

Khurshid Ahmad (ed) — *Islam - Its Meaning and Message*
Islamic Council of Europe, News and Media Ltd, 33 Stroud Green Rd, London N4 3R7.

Sayyed Hossein Nasr — *Ideals and Realities of Islam*
George Allen & Unwin (1968), 184 pp.

M. Y. McDermott and M. M. Alison — *The Muslim Guide for Teachers, Employers, Community Workers and Social Administrators in Britain*
Islamic Foundation, Leicester (1980), 104 pp.

A wide range of literature is available (sometimes free) from Islamic Cultural Centres which have been established in many countries; eg,

Islamic Cultural Centre, Regent's Lodge, 146 Park Road, London NW8
The Islamic Foundation, 223 London Rd, Leicester LE2 1ZE
Islamic Book Centre (UK Islamic Mission), 148 Liverpool Rd, London N1
Islamic Center, 2551 Massachusetts Ave, NW, Washington, DC.

General Books on Islam

Harry R. Boer — *A Brief History of Islam*
Daystar Press, Box 1261, Ibadan, Nigeria (1950), 208 pp.

Harry R. Boer — *A Brief History of Islam*
A Christian Interpretation.
Daystar Press, Box 1261, Ibadan, Nigeria (1968), 121 pp.

Norman Anderson (ed) — *The World's Religions*
Inter Varsity Press
Contains an excellent chapter on Islam by Professor Anderson.

Alfred Guillaume — *Islam*
Penguin (1954), 207 pp.
One of the best studies of the origin and development of Islam by a western orientalist.

John B. Taylor — *Introducing Islam*
Lutterworth, 63 pp.
A helpful, illustrated introduction, prepared as a textbook for schools.

David Brown — *The Way of the Prophet*
Highway Press, Church Missionary Society
An excellent introduction to the life of the Prophet.

W. Montgomery Watt — *Muhammad, Prophet and Statesman*
Oxford University Press, 250 pp.
A scholarly but very readable study of the life of Muhammad.

Kenneth Cragg — *The House of Islam*
Dickenson, USA.

Kenneth Cragg — *Islam and the Muslim*
Textbook for the Open University
Open University Press (1979).

Kenneth Cragg — *Alive to God*
An Anthology of Muslim and Christian prayer.
OUP (1970), 194 pp.

Kenneth Cragg — *Counsels in Contemporary Islam*
Edinburgh University Press (1965).

Kenneth Cragg and Marston Speight — *Islam From Within: Anthology of a Religion*
Wadsworth (1980).

H. A. R. Gibb — *Islam,* An Historical Survey
Oxford University Press (1969), 144 pp.

W. Cantwell Smith — *Islam in Modern History*
Mentor Books, New American Library (1957), 310 pp.
A valuable book, dealing with some of the challenges (especially political) facing different Islamic countries.

W. Montgomery Watt — *Companion to the Qur'an*
George Allen & Unwin (1967), 355 pp.

Christian Witness to Islam

Margaret Burness — *What would you say if . . .?*
Africa Christian Press (1980).

Kenneth Cragg — *The Call of the Minaret*
Oxford University Press (1956), 376 pp.
Cragg's first book, which has perhaps influenced Christian thinking about Islam more than any other book in the last 20 years.

Kenneth Cragg — *Sandals at the Mosque, Christian Presence Amid Islam*
SCM Press (1959), 160 pp.

Phil Parshall — *The Fortress and the Fire, Jesus Christ and the Challenge of Islam*
Gospel Literature Service, Bombay (1976), 134 pp.

Phil Parshall — *New Paths in Muslim Evangelism: Evangelical Approaches to Contextualisation*
Baker (1981).

William Miller — *A Christian Response to Islam*
Presbyterian & Reformed Publishing Co, Nutley, New Jersey (1977), 175 pp.

David Brown — *A New Threshold,* Guidelines for the Churches in their Relations with Muslim Communities

British Council of Churches and the Conference of British Missionary Societies (1976), 41 pp. Now out of print.

Don McCurry (ed) — *The Gospel and Islam*
Compendium of the Colorado Springs Conference on Muslim Evangelism (1978)

An invaluable collection of study papers covering many of the issues related to Christian witness to Islam.

Jens Christensen — *The Practical Approach to Muslims*
reprinted by North Africa Mission (1977) 644 pp.

Christian Witness to Muslims

Report of the 1980 COWE Consultation on Reaching Muslims at Pattaya, Thailand, published as Lausanne Occasional Paper.

Missiology, Quarterly Journal, Vol IV, number 3 July 1976

Contains many valuable articles on different aspects of Christian mission to Islam today.

Colin Chapman — *Thinking Biblically About Islam*
Article in *Themelios* (International journal for theological students) (April 1978, published by IFES, 10 College Rd, Harrow, England.

Biography, Autobiography & Historical Studies

Bilquis Sheikh — *I Dared to Call Him Father*
Kingsway Publications (1978), 190 pp

A moving story of a Pakistani woman's pilgrimage to faith.

C. R. Marsh
Too Hard For God?

C. R. Marsh
Streams in the Sahara
Echoes of Service, 1 Widecombe Crescent, Bath, England.

Based on the author's life-time of service in North Africa.

William Miller
Ten Muslims Meet Christ
Eerdmans (1969), 147 pp.

Mark Hanna
The True Path, Seven Muslims Make Their Greatest Discovery. International Doorways Publishers, Colorado Springs.

Roger Hooker
Uncharted Journey
Church Missionary Society (1973)

Includes an excellent chapter on dialogue with Muslims in India.

Patrick Sookhdeo
Asians in Britain, A Christian Understanding
Falcon Press, CPAS (1972)

Avery T. Willis
Indonesian Revival,
Why Two Million Muslims Came to Christ
William Carey Library, 533 Hermosa St, South Pasadena.

Lyle L. Vander Werff
Christian Missions to Muslims, The Record
William Carey Library (1977), 365 pp.

A detailed, scholarly study comparing Anglican and Reformed Approaches to Islam in India and the Middle East between 1800 and 1938.

David Bentley-Taylor
Weathercock's Reward,
Christian Progress in Muslim Java, OMF (1975), 148 pp.

David Bentley-Taylor
My Love Must Wait, the Story of Henry Martyn, Inter Varsity Press (1975). 160 pp.

Paul Hunt
Inside Iran
Lion Publishing (1981).

Evelyn Stenbock
Miss Terri
Gospel Missionary Union, Smithville, Missouri, 64089 (1970).

A study of the early work of this mission in Morocco.

Phyllis Thompson

Minka and Margaret
Hodder and Stoughton and OMF (1976)

The story of two OMF women missionaries who were martyred while working among Malay Muslims in South Thailand.

Material for Muslims

Individual gospels and Scripture Selections in many different languages are available from the *Bible Societies.*

Scripture Selections for Muslims are published by the Scripture Gift Mission, Radstock House, 3 Eccleston St, London SW1W 9LZ.

eg, *"The Glory of Christ"* - Selections for Muslims

Dennis E. Clark

The Life and Teaching of Jesus the Messiah
Dove Publications, Elgin, ILL 60120, USA, 200 pp. (also available in Arabic and Urdu).

An excellent life of Christ, written by a missionary in Pakistan who understands the Muslim mind and knows how to explain the gospel to a Muslim.

Iskander Jadid
and others

A wide range of booklets is available in English, Arabic and other languages, written for the Muslim, and dealing with vital subjects like the Trinity, Corruption of the Bible, the Crucifixion, the Atonement etc., from Call of Hope, 7000 Stuttgart 1, PO Box 1018, West Germany.
or The Good Way, CH - 8486 Rikon, PO Box 66, Switzerland.

David Brown

Christianity and Islam Series
(Christian Beliefs Explained to Muslim Readers), Sheldon Press
1. Jesus and God, 1967
2. The Christian Scriptures, 1967
3. The Cross of the Messiah, 1968
4. The Divine Trinity, 1968

Gordon Huelin

5. The Church and the Churches, 1970.